SpringerBriefs in Economics

Kobe University Social Science Research Series

The Kobe University Social Science Research Series has been established as a subseries of the SpringerBrief in Economics Series, but in fact this exciting interdisciplinary collection encompasses scholarly research not only in the economics but also in law, political science, business and management, accounting, international relations, and other subdisciplines within the social sciences. As a national university with a special strength in the social sciences, Kobe University actively promotes interdisciplinary research. This series is not limited only to research emerging from Kobe University's faculties of social sciences but also welcomes cross-disciplinary research that integrates studies in the arts and sciences.

Kobe University, founded in 1902, is the second oldest national higher education institution for commerce in Japan and is now a preeminent institution for social science research and education in the country. Currently, the social sciences section includes four faculties—Law, Economics, Business Administration, and International Cooperation Studies—and the Research Institute for Economics and Business Administration (RIEB). There are some 230-plus researchers who belong to these faculties and conduct joint research through the Center for Social Systems Innovation and the Organization for Advanced and Integrated Research, Kobe University.

This book series comprises academic works by researchers in the social sciences at Kobe University as well as their collaborators at affiliated institutions, Kobe University alumni and their colleagues, and renowned scholars from around the world who have worked with academic staff at Kobe University. Although traditionally the research of Japanese scholars has been publicized mainly in the Japanese language, Kobe University strives to promote publication and dissemination of works in English in order to further contribute to the global academic community.

More information about this series at http://www.springer.com/series/15423

Hideyuki Adachi · Kazuyuki Inagaki ·
Tamotsu Nakamura · Yasuyuki Osumi

Technological Progress, Income Distribution, and Unemployment

Theory and Empirics

Springer

Hideyuki Adachi
Kobe University
Kobe, Hyōgo, Japan

Kazuyuki Inagaki
Nagoya City University
Nagoya, Aichi, Japan

Tamotsu Nakamura
Kobe University
Kobe, Hyōgo, Japan

Yasuyuki Osumi
University of Hyogo
Kobe, Hyōgo, Japan

ISSN 2191-5504 ISSN 2191-5512 (electronic)
SpringerBriefs in Economics
ISSN 2520-1697 ISSN 2520-1700 (electronic)
Kobe University Social Science Research Series
ISBN 978-981-13-3725-3 ISBN 978-981-13-3726-0 (eBook)
https://doi.org/10.1007/978-981-13-3726-0

Library of Congress Control Number: 2018964239

This Springer imprint is published by the registered company Springer Nature Singapore Pte Ltd.
The registered company address is: 152 Beach Road, #21-01/04 Gateway East, Singapore 189721, Singapore

Preface

Technological progress has played a central role in economic growth, income distribution, and unemployment. Macroeconomics, both theories and empirics, has so far shed light on different aspects of this role, using various models. In those models, *neutrality* of technological progress has been one of the key concepts. Once neutrality is defined, the concept of *biased* technological change is correspondingly derived. In the early days of modern growth theory, several different definitions of neutrality were proposed, such as Harrod neutrality, Hicks neutrality, and Solow neutrality. Among these definitions, Harrod neutrality has been commonly used in growth theories, since it is compatible with the balanced growth that is regarded as consistently explaining the observed pattern of long-run economic growth in advanced countries. Due to the Robinson–Uzawa theorem, only purely labor-augmenting technological progress, which amounts to a case of Harrod neutrality, is compatible with balanced growth unless the elasticity of substitution between labor and capital is equal to unity. Thus, most of the literature on growth theories and empirics has focused on the case of Harrod neutrality (i.e., purely labor-augmenting technological progress) or the unitary elasticity of substitution, and has paid little attention to biased technological changes.

Ignited by sharp increases in wage and income inequalities since the beginning of the new century, many macroeconomists have begun to realize the importance of biased technological changes, such as factor-biased, sector-biased, and ability-biased. Among factor-biased technological changes, skill-biased changes are of particular importance in understanding the development of wage inequalities, while capital- and/or labor-biased changes are of great significance in explaining shifts in income distribution between labor and capital. The replacement of human labor with machines as a result of factor-biased technological changes creates downward pressure on wages and upward pressure on unemployment. Of course, the elasticity of substitution between labor and capital plays a crucial role in this replacement. If we examine the influences of factor-biased technological changes on growth, income distribution, and unemployment, we cannot avoid analyzing the role of elasticity. Nevertheless, little theoretical investigation has been carefully carried out concerning what dynamics in income distribution and/or employment emerge as a result of the combined effect of biased technological progress and a non-unit elasticity of substitution between capital and labor.

Even when considering factor-biased technological changes with capital and labor as factors of production, it is usually assumed that labor-augmenting and/or capital-augmenting technological changes occur at nonnegative rates. Put differently, it is supposed a priori that technological progress must increase the efficiency of each physical unit of production factors: capital or labor. However, a type of technological progress can exist that rapidly increases the efficiency of labor but decreases the efficiency of capital, possibly slightly. In fact, labor-saving technological progress under Harrod's criterion is characterized as this type. When labor is scarce, and the wage rate is high, it will be more profitable for a firm to choose this type of technological progress instead of that which slightly increases the efficiency of both capital and labor. In other words, the firm prefers technology that saves a great deal of labor and uses more capital to that which saves both capital and labor by a small amount. It is surprising to exclude in advance the possibility of factor-*reducing* technological progress, although the type of technological progress is endogenously determined mainly via R&D investment by firms. Even more surprisingly, few empirical studies exist to test whether technological progress is factor-augmenting or factor-reducing.

This small volume, which is comprised of five chapters, challenges the perceived notions stated above. Chapter 1 analyzes the effects of biased technological progress on growth and income distribution and shows that long-run trends of the capital/income ratio and capital share of income emerge when technological progress is labor saving and the elasticity of substitution between labor and capital is below unity, consistent with Piketty's (2014) empirical results. Incorporating the modified version of induced innovation theory, which yields various types of technological progress, into standard neoclassical growth, Chap. 2 explains the long-run fluctuations of growth and income distribution consistent with the data shown in Piketty (2014). Introducing a wage-setting function, Chap. 3 extends the neoclassical growth model to account for unemployment and examines the dynamics of unemployment and the labor share of income under biased technological progress and various elasticities of substitution between capital and labor. Applying a new econometric method to Japanese industrial data, Chap. 4 tests the key assumptions employed and important results derived in the previous chapters, and, as a result, shows that the following are relevant and empirically justified: (1) the elasticity of substitution between capital and labor is less than unity, and (2) labor-saving and capital-using technological progress has existed for the past two decades.

Kobe, Japan — Hideyuki Adachi
Nagoya, Japan — Kazuyuki Inagaki
Kobe, Japan — Tamotsu Nakamura
Kobe, Japan — Yasuyuki Osumi

Acknowledgements

This volume was born from a workshop series on medium and long-run macroeconomics of growth and income distribution. The series has been organized mainly by President and Prof. Takeshi Nakatani and Prof. Shin Imoto of the Onomichi City University. Hence, our special thanks go first to the two macroeconomists for their devotion and stimulating comments in the workshops. We are also grateful to the many active and regular participants for their invaluable inputs to this volume, including in particular Profs. Taro Abe (Nagoya Gakuin University), Katsufumi Fukuda (Hiroshima University), Atsushi Miyake (Kobe Gakuin University), Junpei Tanaka (Kitakyushu City University), Yasutaka Tsunehiro (Kobe Gakuin University), and Kenji Yamashita (Okayama Shoka University). Of course, we are solely responsible for any remaining errors.

The financial support of Grants-in-Aid for Scientific Research from the Japan Society for the Promotion of Science (15K03431, 16K03555, and 17K18564) is gratefully acknowledged. Also, the authors would like to thank the Kobe University Center for Social Systems Innovation and the Kobe Academic Park Association for the Promotion of Inter-University Research and Exchange for their financial assistance.

Last, but not least, our thanks are also due to Prof. Takashi Yanagawa of Kobe University, the editor of this brief series, who has encouraged us to publish our findings as one of the series.

Contents

Chapter 1
Growth and Income Distribution Under Biased Technological Progress

Abstract Instead of focusing on the case of neutral technological progress as in conventional growth models, we investigate the role of biased technological progress in economic growth and income distribution, using the neoclassical growth model. It is shown that Piketty's (Capital in the twenty-first century. Belknap Press of Harvard University Press, Cambridge, 2014) empirical results regarding the long-run trends of the capital/income ratio and capital share of income are consistently explained by biased technological progress with the elasticity of substitution between labor and capital less than unity. The "productivity paradox" pointed out by Solow is also shown to be explained as a case of labor-saving technological progress. The conditions under which firms have incentives to introduce labor-saving (or capital-saving) technological progress are also investigated. If firms choose a technology type to increase the rate of return on capital, labor-saving (or capital-saving) technological progress is introduced when the labor share of income exceeds (or falls short of) the elasticity of substitution between labor and capital. The introduction of labor-saving (or capital-saving) technological progress lowers (or raises) the labor share of income, which as a result is adjusted towards the value of the elasticity of substitution between labor and capital.

Keywords Harrod's criterion on technological progress
Labor-saving (capital-saving) technological progress
Elasticity of substitution between labor and capital · Capital share of income
Capital/output ratio

1.1 Introduction

Throughout human history, technological progress has exerted a major influence on the economy, as well as on society and culture. The recent remarkable technological breakthroughs over a wide range of fields, such as artificial intelligence (AI), robot technology, biotechnology, and others, will have significant impact on the global economy in the future. In this chapter, we examine the effects of techno-

H. Adachi et al., *Technological Progress, Income Distribution, and Unemployment*, Kobe University Social Science Research Series,
https://doi.org/10.1007/978-981-13-3726-0_1

logical progress on the macro economy, especially focusing on its effects on economic growth and income distribution. The effects of technological progress on economic growth and income distribution have so far been analyzed using various types of growth models, particularly the neo-classical model, represented by the Solow growth model.[1] However, most such models deal with the case of neutral technological progress and the steady state equilibrium is achieved. The case of biased technological progress has rarely been examined by the literature on growth and income distribution. This is because the property of the steady state equilibrium, where the values of the variables rise together, is regarded as doing a good job of describing the long-run data for the U.S., the U.K., and many other advanced economies. The empirical facts demonstrated by these long-run data, including the constancy of the capital-output ratio and the capital share of income (or labor share of income) are called the stylized facts of capitalist development, first proposed by Kaldor.[2] Thus, it is asserted that the steady state of the neoclassical growth model with neutral technological progress can consistently explain the stylized facts of capitalist development. However, recent empirical studies conducted by Piketty (2014) found that the capital-output ratio and capital share of income for some advanced countries do not stay constant, but secularly alternate rising and falling phases, thus refuting the stylized facts of capitalist development.[3] In particular, he found that in the rising phase of the capital-output ratio, the rate of return on capital is falling and the capital share of income is rising; the opposite holds in the falling phase of the capital-output ratio. To explain these secular rises or falls in the capital-output ratio and the capital share of income, Piketty had to assume the elasticity of substitution between labor and capital to be greater than unity.[4] However, many empirical studies have shown the elasticity of substitution to be less than unity.[5] Thus, assuming the elasticity of substitution to be less than unity, the problem of explaining Piketty's empirical results remains. It will be shown in this chapter that this problem is solved if we consider the effects of biased technological progress in the growth model.

In this chapter, we propose a growth model that includes factor-biased technological progress (both labor-saving and capital-saving) and show that Piketty's empirical results can consistently be explained when the elasticity of substitution is less than unity. It will also be shown that the size of the elasticity of substitution relative to that of the labor share of income is crucial in determining the type of technological progress chosen by firms . If the elasticity of substitution is less than unity and

---

[1] See Solow (1956).

[2] See Kaldor (1961).

[3] See Piketty (2014), Part Two: The Dynamics of the Capital/Income Ratio, pp. 113–234.

[4] See Piketty (2014), pp. 220–222.

[5] The empirical studies by Chirinko (2008), Oberfield and Raval (2014), Chirinko and Mallick (2017), and Lawrence (2015) have all provided results showing that the elasticity of substitution is less than unity. In his comments on Piketty's book, Summers (2014) points out that Piketty's argument that factor substitution elasticity is above 1 may stem from confusion between gross and net returns to capital. Since the return net of depreciation is relevant, he argues, output should be measured in net terms, and then the elasticity of substitution is likely below 1.

smaller than the labor share of income, labor-saving technological progress becomes dominant, causing a decline in the labor share of income and a fall in the real wage rate as a result.

The rest of this chapter is organized as follows. Section 1.2 summarizes Piketty's empirical results and refers to some critical comments on his results, then reviews his theoretical explanation of long-term fluctuations in the capital-output ratio and income distribution and points out its problems. In Sect. 1.3, we introduce a neoclassical growth model that includes factor-augmenting technological progress in the production function, and classify technological progress based on Harrod's criterion. Then, in the case of neutral technological progress, it is shown that the elasticity of substitution must be greater than unity for Piketty's empirical results to be supported, so this case is inconsistent with the empirical studies on the elasticity of substitution. Section 1.4 deals with the case of biased technological progress. It is shown that each phase of long-term fluctuations in the capital-output ratio and income distribution can be explained by labor-saving or capital-saving technological progress with the elasticity of substitution less than unity, which is the empirically supported result. In Sect. 1.5, we investigate the condition under which firms choose to introduce biased technological progress and then examine their effects on macroeconomic variables. The value of the elasticity of substitution relative to the labor share of income is shown to be crucial for the type of technological progress chosen by the firm. Finally, Sect. 1.6 concludes the chapter.

1.2 Long-Term Fluctuations in Income Distribution—Piketty's Empirical Results and Theoretical Explanation

1.2.1 Piketty's Empirical Results

Capital in the 21st Century (2014), written by Thomas Piketty, highlights the dynamics of the inequality of income and wealth distribution in some advanced countries, and changed economists' understanding of this problem. This work is based on empirical research conducted by Piketty and his collaborators over more than a decade, drawing on investigations of a massive amount of data, including many countries and extending over several centuries. There is the well-known contribution by Simon Kuznets in this type of work,[6] but the period of the data and number of countries in Piketty's study are vastly greater than those of Kuznets' work. In addition, Piketty's work features many new discoveries about long-term fluctuations in macroeconomic variables, including the distribution of income and wealth.

[6]See Kuznets (1955).

In an influential paper, Kaldor (1961) pointed out that long-term growth of a capitalist economy can be summarized by the following properties.[7] (1) Aggregate output and labor productivity show continuing growth with no tendency for a decline in the growth rate of productivity. (2) Capital stock per worker shows continuing growth. (3) The rate of return on capital is steady. (4) The capital/output ratio is steady. (5) Labor and capital receive constant shares of total income. (6) There are wide differences in the rate of growth of productivity across countries.

The observations summarized above have been called the "stylized facts of capitalist development," and it has been presumed that growth theory must explain these facts without contradiction. Neoclassical growth theory, as represented by Solow's growth model, has made it clear that these stylized facts can be explained as the steady state equilibrium of the model. As a result, the "stylized facts of capitalism" have been treated as if they are established truth, and growth theory has been preoccupied with analysis of the steady state equilibrium. However, these stylized facts are not necessarily based on rigorous research using empirical data. Instead, they seem to be conjectured from the sustainability conditions of the capitalist economy. For example, since an economy in which the rate of return on capital and capital share of income decline permanently will become unsustainable, these variables must rise sooner or later for the economy to be sustainable. Thus, it is maintained that these variables must be constant in the long-run. However, explaining how long the long-run is remains a problem.

In comparison to these stylized facts, Piketty's empirical data summarize historical facts and tendencies with more accuracy and sufficiency. Piketty found, based on long-term data from 1700 to 2010, that the following tendencies are observed for the capital/output ratio (capital/income ratio), capital share of income, and rate of return on capital in France and England.[8] (1) The capital/output ratio was more or less stable at a constant level through the 18th and 19th centuries, but fell from the beginning of the 20th century (around 1910) to its middle (around 1950), and then rose to the beginning of the 21st century (2010). (2) The capital share of income exhibited more or less the same movement as the capital/output ratio, but the decline from the beginning to the middle of the 20th century and the rise from the middle of the 20th century to the beginning of the 21st century are more modest than those of the capital/output ratio. (3) The rate of return on capital was more or less constant through the 18th and 19th centuries but rose from the beginning to the middle of the 20th century and fell from then to the beginning of the 21st century (2010).

Furthermore, Piketty provides data on the capital/income ratios for 1970–2010 and the capital share of income for 1975–2010 in eight rich countries. In all eight countries, the capital/income ratios and capital share of income exhibit a tendency to rise secularly, while showing short-term fluctuations. Piketty predicts that this tendency will likely continue in the future.[9]

---

[7] See Kaldor (1961), pp. 177–222.

[8] See Piketty (2014), pp. 164–234.

[9] Jones (2016) reports that the ratio of physical capital to output in the US has remained nearly constant since 1945, while the shares of capital and labor in total factor payments were quite stable

In short, Piketty has shown that the capital/income ratio and capital share of income exhibit a tendency to rise or fall over considerably long periods, so that "the stylized facts of capitalist development" may not hold. To summarize his observations, the rate of return on capital varies in the opposite direction of the capital/output rate, while the capital share of income varies in the same direction as the capital/output rate. Given this, how is such movement in the macro variables explained? As Piketty argues, the fact that a rise in the capital/output rate results in a fall in the rate of return on capital can be explained by the diminishing marginal productivity of capital caused by capital accumulation. However, to explain the rise in the capital share of income at the same time, it is necessary to assume that the elasticity of substitution between capital and labor must be greater than 1. Piketty argues that the elasticity of substitution of capital and labor is actually greater than 1.

However, many empirical studies have shown the elasticity of substitution between capital and labor to be below 1. Empirical studies by Chirinko (2008), Oberfield and Raval (2014), Chirinko and Mallick (2017), and Lawrence (2015) have all produced these results. In his comments on Piketty's study, Summers (2014) argues that the rising capital share of income should be attributed to technological change and globalization rather than attributing it to the process of capital accumulation. For example, he notes that mechanization of what was previously manual work will raise the capital share of income, as does the greater ability to make use of low-cost foreign labor.[10]

In the following sections, we analyze the effects of technological change on income distribution by constructing a growth model that includes biased technological progress. It is shown that if bias in technological progress is considered, the observed fact that the capital share of income rises or falls with the capital/output ratio can be explained even if the elasticity of factor substitution is below 1. In addition, we show that it is profitable for firms to introduce biased technological progress under certain conditions, so that the introduction of biased technological progress is endogenously determined.[11]

---

between 1948 and 2000. Since around 2000, however, "there has been a marked decline in labor share and a corresponding rise in capital income." Homburg (2015) criticizes Piketty for equating wealth with capital. He argues that Piketty's wealth includes not only capital goods in the sense of produced means of production, but also land and other natural resources, and that the observed increase in the wealth-income ratio reflects rising prices of land and natural resources. Similar criticism is made by Blume and Durlauf (2015). In the theoretical model we present, capital means capital goods in the sense of produced means of production.

[10]See Summers (2014).

[11]By incorporating endogenous schooling, Grossman et al. (2017) present a growth model that converges to a balanced growth path even in the presence of capital-augmenting technological progress. Their argument assumes that capital-augmenting technological progress must be positive. However, we will show in this chapter that negative capital-augmenting technological progress could be chosen by firms because it is profitable. Moreover, the empirical study in Chap. 4 shows that negative capital-augmenting technology normally happens.

1.2.2 Piketty's Theoretical Explanation[12]

Piketty argues that the dynamics of the main macro variables, such as those described above, can be explained by two fundamental laws of capitalism. The first is the formula of identity that relates the capital-income ratio K/Y to the capital share of income θ_K via the rate of return on capital r as follows:

$$\theta_K = r \times \frac{K}{Y}. \tag{1.1}$$

The second is the formula that relates the capital/income ratio K/Y to the savings rate s and the growth rate of capital stock g:

$$\frac{K}{Y} = \frac{s}{g}. \tag{1.2}$$

With these fundamental laws of capitalism, Piketty's theoretical explanation goes as follows. If g in Eq. (1.2) declines, K/Y increases as long as s remains constant. When K/Y increases, the rate of return on capital r declines. Here, if the rate of decline in r is smaller than the rate of increase in K/Y, the capital share of income θ_K increases, as is clear from Eq. (1.1). This happens if the decrease in marginal productivity of capital is small enough; that is to say, the elasticity of substitution between labor and capital is above 1. Thus, if the elasticity of substitution is above 1, the decline in the growth rate g of capital results in an increase in the capital/output ratio and in the capital share of income. Piketty argues that the elasticity of substitution tends to be greater than 1 over a very long period, because there are many different uses of capital in the long-run.

Thus, Piketty has provided a simple theory that explains his empirical findings. However, as noted above, most empirical studies on the elasticity of substitution between labor and capital have shown its value to be below 1. If this is the case, Piketty's theoretical explanation is not supported. In the next section, we develop a growth model that includes biased technological progress to resolve this inconsistency.

[12]See Piketty (2014), pp. 212–227.

1.3 Analysis of Growth and Income Distribution Based on the Neoclassical Growth Model

1.3.1 A Neoclassical Growth Model Including Biased Technological Progress

In Piketty's definition of the capital/income ratio, income Y means national income, which is defined as gross domestic product (GDP) minus depreciation plus income received from abroad. In the following discussion, a closed economy is assumed for simplicity, so that income received from abroad is ignored. Thus, national income Y is equal to the net domestic product. Let us assume that national income Y as defined is determined by the following production function:

$$Y = F(AN, BK), \tag{1.3}$$

where N is the amount of labor, K is capital stock, A is the efficiency coefficient of labor, and B is the efficiency coefficient of capital. In this production function, both the efficiency coefficient of labor and the efficiency coefficient of capital are explicitly introduced to make it possible to deal with biased technological change as well as neutral technology. If the production function is linearly homogeneous, it is rewritten as follows:

$$y = f(k) \quad where \ y \equiv \frac{Y}{AN}, \quad k \equiv \frac{BK}{AN}. \tag{1.4}$$

This production function in the ratio form is assumed to have the ordinary well-behaved properties such as $f' > 0$ and $f'' < 0$. To focus on the analysis of technological progress, we adopt the simplest assumptions concerning saving and consumption behavior and assume that a constant percentage s of income is saved. Then, total saving S is expressed as follows:

$$S = sY. \tag{1.5}$$

With this saving function, the equality of saving and investment is expressed by the following equation:

$$g = sB\frac{f(k)}{k}, \tag{1.6}$$

where g represents the growth rate of capital stock $\dot{K}/K$. Here and in the following $\dot{x} \equiv dx/dt$ for any variable x and time t. We assume that labor is fully employed, and the working population increases at a constant rate λ. As for technological progress, we first consider the case where it is exogenously determined and examine the effects of biased technological progress on the main macro variables. Representing the growth rate of the efficiency coefficient of labor A by α and the efficiency coefficient of capital B by β, we assume that they are exogenously given. In this case, the time change rate of the capital/labor ratio in efficiency unit k is given by

$$\dot{k}/k = g + \beta - \alpha - \lambda, \tag{1.7}$$

where

$$\lambda \equiv \dot{N}/N, \quad \alpha \equiv \dot{A}/A, \quad \beta \equiv \dot{B}/B. \tag{1.8}$$

The time paths of k and g are determined by (1.6) and (1.7).[13]

Under firms' profit maximizing behavior, the demand for capital and labor are determined such that the marginal productivity of capital is equal to the real interest rate r, and the marginal productivity of labor is equal to the real wage rate w, which are expressed by the following equations:

$$r = Bf'(k), \tag{1.9}$$

$$w = A\{f(k) - kf'(k)\}. \tag{1.10}$$

Therefore, the capital share of income is

$$\theta_K = \frac{rK}{Y} = \frac{kf'(k)}{f(k)}, \quad where \ 0 < \theta_K < 1, \tag{1.11}$$

and the capital/output ratio is

$$\frac{K}{Y} = \frac{k}{Bf(k)}. \tag{1.12}$$

As noted above, when the time path of k is determined from (1.6) and (1.7), the time paths of r, w, θ_K, and K/Y are also determined.

1.3.2 *Classification of Technological Progress*

Technological progress in an economy is usually measured by total factor productivity (TFP), which is calculated by dividing total output by the weighted average of factor inputs (labor and capital in this case). It is expressed as $\theta\alpha + (1-\theta)\beta$ when

---

[13] A growth model in which both labor-augmenting progress α and capital-augmenting progress β are considered has been studied by Vanek (1966). However, he focuses on the dynamics of the growth rates of capital and output and does not examine the dynamics of factor prices and income distribution. Moreover, he assumes that $\alpha \geq 0$ and $\beta \geq 0$. He does not consider the case $\beta < 0$, which is classified as labor-saving technological progress due to Harrod's criterion as seen below.

the production function is given by (1.3). Assuming this value to be positive, the types of technological progress are classified according to their effects on income distribution. There are different criteria for classifying technological progress due to differences in the definition of neutrality. However, in growth theory, Harrod's criterion is commonly used, because it is suitable for analyzing economic growth.[14] Under Harrod's criterion, the steady state equilibrium, which plays a central role in growth theory, is achieved when technological progress is neutral. To classify biased technological progress based on this criterion for neutrality seems to be quite appropriate.

Harrod's criterion for classifying the types of technological progress is stated as follows. Technological progress is defined as neutral if, for a given real rate of interest (=the rate of return on capital), technological progress maintains a constant capital/output ratio, and it is labor-saving or capital-saving depending on whether it causes the capital/output ratio to rise or fall.

This criterion is interpreted as follows. Technological progress that maintains a constant capital/output ratio K/Y for a given real interest rate r (=the rate of return on capital), also maintains a constant capital cost per unit of output rK/Y and, therefore, constant labor cost per unit of output wN/Y. In this case, technological progress does not affect the cost structure, so it is defined as neutral technological progress. Next, technological progress that increases the capital/output ratio K/Y for a given rate of return on capital r involves a rise in rK/Y, thus causing wN/Y to fall, so it is defined as labor-saving technological progress. Conversely, technological progress that lowers K/Y for r involves a decline in rK/Y, causing wN/Y to rise, so it is defined as capital-saving technological progress.[15]

Applying Harrod's criterion to the above model, we next examine how factor-augmenting technological progress expressed by (1.3) is classified into labor-saving or capital-saving. Taking the rate of changes in the real interest rate (1.9) and the capital/output ratio (1.12), we have

$$\frac{\dot{r}}{r} = \beta - \frac{1-\theta_K}{\sigma}\frac{\dot{k}}{k}, \tag{1.13a}$$

$$\frac{\dot{K}}{K} - \frac{\dot{Y}}{Y} = (1-\theta_K)\frac{\dot{k}}{k} - \beta, \tag{1.13b}$$

---

[14] See Harrod (1948). Besides Harrod's criterion, Hicks' criterion is also well-known. Hicks defines neutral technological progress as that which raises the marginal productivity of labor and capital equally with any given capital/labor ratio. However, this neutrality is built within the framework of static analysis and is not suitable for analyzing a growth process in which the capital/labor ratio is constantly changing.

[15] While labor-saving technological progress causes labor cost per unit of output to relatively decline, it causes capital cost per unit of output to rise, so it can also be called capital-using technological progress. Robinson (1956) employed the term capital-using technological progress instead of labor-saving technological progress. Similarly, capital-saving technological progress can also be called labor-using technological progress. In this book, the terms labor-saving technological progress and capital-saving technological progress are used.

where θ_K is the capital share of income defined by (1.11), and σ is the elasticity of substitution between capital and labor, which is defined as follows[16]:

$$\sigma \equiv -\frac{dk/k}{d(r/w)/(r/w)} = -\frac{f'(k)\{f(k) - kf'(k)\}}{kf(k)f''(k)}. \tag{1.14}$$

From (1.13a), the condition for the real interest rate to be constant is given by

$$\frac{\dot{k}}{k} = \frac{\sigma}{1-\theta_K}\beta. \tag{1.15}$$

Substituting this equation into (1.13b), we can calculate the rate of change of the capital/output ratio for a given real interest rate as follows:

$$\frac{\dot{K}}{K} - \frac{\dot{Y}}{Y} = (\sigma - 1)\beta \tag{1.16}$$

In view of Harrod's criterion mentioned above, technological progress is neutral, labor-saving, or capital-saving depending on whether $(\sigma - 1)\beta$ is zero, positive, or negative. Thus, we obtain the following proposition:

Proposition 1.1 *(Classification of technological progress) Suppose that technological progress is factor-augmenting and the growth rate of total factor productivity is positive, that is,* $(1 - \theta_K)\alpha + \theta_K \beta > 0$*. Then, technological progress is classified by Harrod's criterion as follows.*

(1) If $\frac{\dot{B}}{B} \equiv \beta = 0$*, technological progress is neutral.*
(2) When $\sigma < 1$*, it is labor-saving if* $\frac{\dot{B}}{B} \equiv \beta < 0$*, and capital-saving if* $\frac{\dot{B}}{B} \equiv \beta > 0$*.*
(3) When $\sigma > 1$*, it is labor-saving if* $\frac{\dot{B}}{B} \equiv \beta > 0$*, and capital-saving if* $\frac{\dot{B}}{B} \equiv \beta < 0$*.*
(4) If $\sigma = 1$*, it is neutral in all cases.*

Based on this classification of technological progress, we first analyze growth and income distribution in the case of neutral technological progress, and then in the case of biased technological progress.

1.3.3 Growth and Income Distribution Under Neutral Technological Progress

Piketty's theoretical explanation of growth and income distribution mentioned above is simply a case of neutral technological progress in the neoclassical growth model. When technological progress is neutral in the neoclassical growth model presented

[16] As definition (1.14) shows, the elasticity of substitution σ is a function of the capital/labor ratio k. In the following discussion, however, we assume it to be constant, which implies that the production function is assumed to be CES.

in Sect. 1.3.1, we can set $\beta = 0$ and $B = 1$ in Eqs. (1.6), (1.7), (1.9), and (1.12). In this case, by taking the time derivative of Eq. (1.6) and substituting (1.7) into it, we have the following dynamic equation with respect to the growth rate of capital g:

$$\dot{g}/g = (1 - \theta_K)(\alpha + \lambda - g). \tag{1.17}$$

Similarly, by taking the time derivative for Eq. (1.11) and taking Eq. (1.14) into account, we have the following dynamic equation with respect to the capital share of income θ_K:

$$\frac{\dot{\theta}_K}{\theta_K} = \frac{1 - \sigma}{\sigma}(1 - \theta_K)(\alpha + \lambda - g), \tag{1.18}$$

where σ is the elasticity of substitution between labor and capital defined by (1.14). The dynamic path of g and θ_K is determined by (1.17) and (1.18). From these two equations, the relationship between the change in the growth rate of capital stock and the change in the capital share of income is clarified.[17]

The steady state equilibrium ($\dot{g} = 0, \dot{\theta}_K = 0$) of this dynamic system is attained when $g = \alpha + \lambda$. This steady state equilibrium is obviously stable. Let us assume that the economy was initially at the steady state equilibrium, and that the growth rate was $g_0 = \alpha_0 + \lambda_0$. Suppose that the steady growth rate has declined to $\alpha_1 + \lambda_1$, owing to a decline in either the rate of technological progress or the population growth rate, or both. Then, we have $g_0 > \alpha_1 + \lambda_1$ and, from Eq. (1.17), $\dot{g} < 0$. Thus, g falls towards the new steady state $\alpha_1 + \lambda_1$. As for θ_K, we have $\dot{\theta}_K > 0$ if $\sigma > 1$, and $\dot{\theta}_K < 0$ if $\sigma < 1$ from (1.18). In other words, if $\sigma > 1$, the capital share of income θ_K rises as g declines, and if $\sigma < 1$, θ_K falls as g falls. Therefore, the capital share of income declines as the growth rate of the economy declines only if $\sigma > 1$, as argued by Piketty.

As for the capital/output ratio, taking the time derivative of Eq. (1.12), we have

$$\dot{K}/K - \dot{Y}/Y = -(1 - \theta_K)(\alpha + \lambda - g). \tag{1.19}$$

As is obvious from this equation, the capital/output ratio rises as the growth rate of capital stock declines. Finally, the rate of change in the real interest rate (=rate of return on capital) and that in the wage rate are derived from (1.9) and (1.10) as follows:

[17] The relationship between the growth rate of capital g and the growth rate of national income g_Y is $g_Y = (1 - \theta_K)(\alpha + \lambda) + \theta_K(g + \beta)$. If $\alpha + \lambda$ and β are taken as given, g_Y also rises (falls) when g rises (falls). Particularly, if technological progress is neutral, $g_Y = g = \alpha + \lambda$ at equilibrium. Therefore, in the following discussion, "growth rate" may be understood as the growth rate of national income as well as the growth rate of capital.

$$\frac{\dot{r}}{r} = \frac{1 - \theta_K}{\sigma}(\alpha + \lambda - g), \tag{1.20}$$

$$\frac{\dot{w}}{w} = \alpha - \frac{\theta_K}{\sigma}(\alpha + \lambda - g). \tag{1.21}$$

Thus, as the growth rate g declines, the rate of return on capital r falls, while the wage rate w rises at a higher rate than the labor-augmenting technological progress rate α. When $\sigma > 1$, the decline in the rate of return on capital r is less than the rise in the capital coefficient K/Y, so the capital share of income θ_K increases as stated above.

The above results may be summarized by a proposition as follows.

Proposition 1.2 *Suppose that the economy with neutral technological progress is initially at the steady state equilibrium, and then the steady growth rate (the sum of technological progress and population growth rates) has fallen. In this case, if the elasticity of substitution between labor and capital is above unity ($\sigma > 1$), then in the transition to the new steady state, the growth rate of capital stock (and national income) falls, and the capital share of income rises. In addition, the capital/output ratio rises, the rate of return on capital falls, and the real wage rate rises. If the elasticity of substitution of labor and capital is below 1 ($\sigma < 1$), the capital share of income falls, but the other results are the same.*

This proposition supports Piketty's argument. However, as previously noted, numerous empirical studies have found that the elasticity of substitution between labor and capital is below unity. In the next section, we show that this problem is solved by introducing biased technological progress.

1.4 Economic Growth and Income Distribution Under Biased Technological Progress

1.4.1 Capital-Labor Substitution: An Elasticity Less Than Unity

To justify his assertion that the elasticity of substitution of labor and capital is above 1 in the long-run, Piketty offers the following intuitive reasoning: "(The) observed historical evolutions suggest that it is always possible–up to a certain point, at least–to find new and useful things to do with capital: for example, new ways of building and equipping houses (think of solar panels on rooftops or digital lighting controls), even more sophisticated robots and other electronic devices, and medical technologies requiring larger and larger capital investments."[18] However, this argument seems to

[18] See Piketty (2014), p. 221.

confuse movement along a given production function with shifts of a production function due to technological progress. The elasticity of substitution between labor and capital is the concept defined for a production function at a given state of technology. When new technologies appear one after another due to technological progress, the total substitution between labor and capital consists of the substitution within a given state of technology and the substitution due to technological progress. In an economy where technological progress is actively taking place, the substitution of the latter may account for a greater part than the substitution of the former. Therefore, the empirical result that the elasticity of substitution between labor and capital is below unity is quite reasonable if we consider labor-saving technological progress.

1.4.2 The Case of Labor-Saving Technological Progress ($\beta < 0$ and $\sigma < 1$)

Let us examine the case of labor-saving technological progress, where $\beta < 0$ and $\sigma < 1$. Taking the time derivative of Eq. (1.6) and substituting Eq. (1.7) into it, we obtain the following dynamic equation for the growth rate of capital stock.

$$\dot{g}/g = (1 - \theta_K)(\alpha + \lambda - g) + \theta_K \beta. \tag{1.22}$$

Similarly, taking the time derivative of Eq. (1.11) and substituting Eq. (1.7) into it, the following dynamic equation for the capital share of income is obtained.

$$\frac{\dot{\theta}_K}{\theta_K} = \frac{1 - \sigma}{\sigma}(1 - \theta_K)[(\alpha + \lambda - g) - \beta]. \tag{1.23}$$

Equations (1.22) and (1.23) above constitute a complete dynamic system for g and θ_K, which determines the paths of these two variables.

To examine the effects of the introduction of labor-saving technological progress, let us assume that the initial economy was at the steady state equilibrium ($g = \alpha + \lambda$) under neutral technological progress ($\beta = 0$). Then, suppose that labor-saving technological progress is introduced ($\beta < 0$). As is obvious from (1.22), this leads to $\dot{g} < 0$, so that the growth rate of capital stock starts to decline. Moreover, from Eq. (1.23), we have $\dot{\theta}_K > 0$ if $\sigma < 1$, which implies that the capital share of income starts to increase. Therefore, if technological progress is labor-saving, we can explain that the capital share of income rises as the growth rate of capital stock declines.

A longer-term analysis may be carried out using a phase diagram. Figure 1.1 depicts the phase diagram of the dynamic system consisting of (1.22) and (1.23) for the case $\sigma < 1$ and $\beta < 0$. If we take θ_K on the horizontal axis and g on the vertical axis, the locus of $\dot{g} = 0$ is depicted by a downward sloping curve that intersects with the vertical axis at $\alpha + \lambda$ and with the horizontal axis at $(\alpha + \lambda)/(\alpha + \lambda - \beta)$. On the other hand, the locus of $\dot{\theta}_K = 0$ is a horizontal line that intersects with the vertical axis at $\alpha + \lambda - \beta$. When $\beta < 0$, the locus of $\dot{\theta}_K = 0$ lies above that of $\dot{g} = 0$,

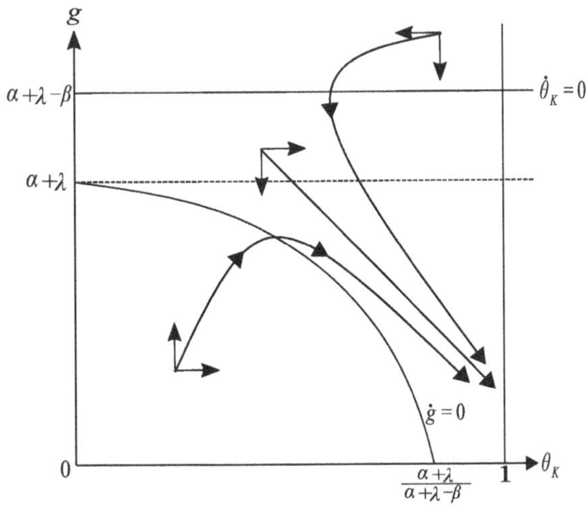

Fig. 1.1 Dynamics of θ_K and g under labor-saving technological progress ($\beta < 0$, $\sigma < 1$)

so that these two loci do not intersect each other. This implies that no steady state equilibrium exists when technological progress is labor-saving. As is clear from this phase diagram, at whatever initial point the dynamic system starts, it enters the phase where the growth rate of capital stock g declines and the capital share of income θ_K rises sooner or later.

A similar analysis can be made for changes in the other variables. The dynamic equation of the capital/output ratio becomes as follows from (1.12) and (1.7):

$$\dot{K}/K - \dot{Y}/Y = -[(1-\theta_K)(\alpha+\lambda-g)+\theta_K\beta]. \tag{1.24}$$

If this equation is compared to Eq. (1.22), it is obvious that the capital/output ratio rises when the growth rate of capital stock declines.

The dynamic equation of the rate of return on capital becomes as follows from (1.13a):

$$\frac{\dot{r}}{r} = \frac{1}{\sigma}[(1-\theta_K)(\alpha+\lambda-g)+\{\sigma-(1-\theta_K)\}\beta]. \tag{1.25}$$

In view of this equation, the introduction of labor-saving technological progress ($\beta < 0$) causes the rate of return on capital to rise ($\dot{r} > 0$) or fall ($\dot{r} < 0$) depending on whether $\sigma < 1-\theta_K$ or $\sigma > 1-\theta_K$; in other words, whether the elasticity of substitution between labor and capital σ is smaller or greater than the share of wages $1-\theta_K$. However, since the capital share of income θ_K continues to rise as shown above, the share of wages $1-\theta_K$ will fall below the elasticity of substitution σ sooner or later. This implies that the rate of return on capital must decline sooner or later under technological progress. Thus, it has been shown that Piketty's empirical finding is consistently explained by introducing labor-saving technological progress even if the elasticity of substitution σ is less than unity.

However, the above model assumes technological progress to be determined exogenously. The problem remains whether it is profitable for firms to introduce labor-saving technological progress. Suppose that the system is initially in the steady state under neutral technological progress ($g = \alpha + \lambda$, $\beta = 0$), and then labor-saving technological progress is introduced ($\beta < 0$). In this case, from Eq. (1.25), we have $\dot{r} > 0$ or $\dot{r} < 0$ depending on whether $\sigma < 1 - \theta_K$ or $\sigma > 1 - \theta_K$. Therefore, if $\sigma < 1 - \theta_K$, the introduction of labor-saving technological progress increases firms' profitability, but if $\sigma > 1 - \theta_K$, the opposite holds. This means that if $\sigma > 1 - \theta_K$, firms may not introduce labor-saving technological progress but may rather introduce capital-saving technological progress ($\beta > 0$). This problem will be discussed in the next section.

The dynamic equation of the wage rate is derived from (1.13) as follows:

$$\frac{\dot{w}}{w} = \alpha - \frac{\theta_K}{\sigma}[(\alpha + \lambda - g) - \beta]. \tag{1.26}$$

If labor-saving technological progress is introduced ($\beta < 0$), and the growth rate of capital stock declines ($g < \alpha + \lambda$), the value in the bracket on the right-hand side of this equation becomes positive, so the rate of the rise in wages falls below the labor-augmenting technological progress rate α, and continues to fall with the decline in the growth rate of capital stock.

The rate of change in labor productivity is calculated from Eq. (1.4) as follows:

$$\dot{Y}/Y - \dot{N}/N = \alpha - \theta_K[(\alpha + \lambda - g) - \beta]. \tag{1.27}$$

As with the growth rate of wages, the growth rate of labor productivity falls below the labor-augmenting technological progress rate α, and continues to fall with the decline in the growth rate of capital stock. Taking the difference between (1.26) and (1.27), it is shown that $\dot{w}/w < \dot{Y}/Y - \dot{N}/N$ as long as $\sigma < 1$. Therefore, under labor-saving technological progress, the growth rate of wages and the growth rate of labor productivity falls, but the former falls below the latter. Thus, labor-saving technological progress brings about stagnation in the growth rates of labor productivity and wages. This result suggests that labor-saving technological progress may become a cause that explains the "productivity paradox" advanced by Robert Solow in the 1980s.[19]

The above results may be summarized by the following proposition.

Proposition 1.3 *Suppose that labor-saving technological progress ($\beta < 0$ under $\sigma < 1$) is introduced in an economy which is initially at steady state equilibrium*

[19]The productivity paradox, which refers to the slowdown in productivity growth in the US in the 1970s and 80s despite rapid development in information technology, is sometimes called the Solow computer paradox in reference to his comment on computers in his article (1987): "You can see the computer age everywhere but in the productivity statistics." There are some arguments that the IT-related productivity jump occurred with delay in the 1990s, and Solow's paradox was resolved. However, Acemoglu et al. (2014) provide some evidence that criticizes the proposed resolutions of Solow's paradox.

under neutral technological progress. The introduction of labor-saving technological progress has the following effects on the main macro variables:

(1) The growth rate of capital stock declines, and the capital share of income rises.
(2) The capital/output ratio rises.
(3) At the beginning, the rate of return on capital rises or falls depending on whether the elasticity of substitution between labor and capital is less or greater than the labor share of income ($\sigma < 1 - \theta_K$ or $\sigma > 1 - \theta_K$). In the long run, the rate of return on capital always falls, since the case $\sigma > 1 - \theta_K$ is realized due to the rise in the capital share of income θ_K.
(4) The growth rates of wages and labor productivity both decline, and in addition, the former falls below the latter.

This proposition shows that Piketty's empirical results are explained as a case of labor-saving technological progress.

1.4.3 The Case of Capital-Saving Technological Progress ($\beta > 0$ and $\sigma < 1$)

Let us next examine the case of capital-saving technological progress, where $\beta > 0$ and $\sigma < 1$. As intuitively conjectured, dynamic changes in the main macro variables under capital-saving technological progress exhibit a tendency just opposite of the case of labor-saving technological progress. In the dynamic system consisting of (1.22) and (1.23), let us assume that the economy is initially at the steady state equilibrium ($g = \alpha + \lambda$) under neutral technological progress ($\beta = 0$), and then capital-saving technological progress ($\beta > 0$) is introduced. We then have $\dot{g} > 0$ and $\dot{\theta}_K < 0$ from those two equations. In other words, if capital-saving technological progress is introduced, the growth rate of capital stock rises, and the capital share of income declines. Figure 1.2 depicts this case using a phase diagram. Starting from the steady state equilibrium P under neutral technological progress, the growth rate of capital stock starts to rise, and the capital share of income starts to decline. In the long run, the growth rate of capital stock turns from the rising phase to the falling phase, but it always exceeds the steady growth rate under neutral technological progress $\alpha + \lambda$. On the other hand, the capital share of income continues to fall through time.

It can be readily seen that with capital-saving technological progress, the capital/output ratio, rate of return on capital, and wage rate generally move inversely to the case of labor-saving technological progress. Therefore, under capital-saving technological progress, the capital share of income falls along with the decline in the capital/output ratio. Thus, capital-saving technological progress can explain the case where the main macro variable changes are opposite of the above described case. The question of under what conditions either labor-saving or capital-saving technological progress is introduced remains to be answered. In Sect. 1.5, we analyze this problem based on the behavior of firms.

Fig. 1.2 Dynamics of θ_K and g under capital-saving technological progress (β >0, σ <1)

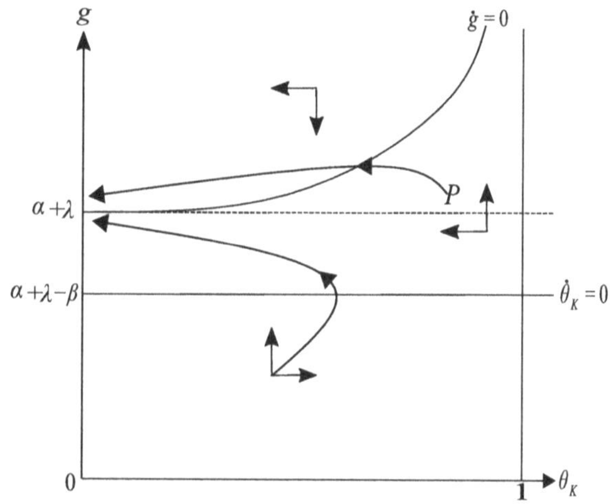

1.4.4 The Case in Which the Elasticity of Substitution Between Labor and Capital σ Is Larger Than Unity

We have discussed the case where the elasticity of substitution σ is below unity. We now examine the case in which σ is above unity. From Proposition 1, in the case where σ >1, technological progress is labor-saving or capital-saving depending on whether $\beta > 0$ or $\beta < 0$. It will be shown below that the dynamic paths in both of these cases cannot adequately explain Piketty's empirical results.

Based on the dynamic system consisting of (1.22) and (1.23), Fig. 1.3 describes the case of labor-saving technological progress ($\beta > 0$ under σ >1). As this phase diagram shows, the growth rate of capital stock g rises without limit, and the capital share of income θ_K also rises to approach unity, regardless of the initial point. In addition, if $\dot{g} > 0$ in (1.22), obviously, $\dot{K}/K - \dot{Y}/Y < 0$ in (1.24), so the capital/output ratio K/Y is declining. Therefore, the capital/output ratio is falling when the growth rate of capital and capital share of income are rising. These trends of the variables are not consistent with Piketty's above mentioned empirical results. The case of capital-saving technological progress (β <0 under σ >1) is depicted in Fig. 1.4 The share of capital income θ_K declines toward zero, while the growth rate of capital stock approaches $\alpha + \lambda$. This case is also not consistent with Piketty's empirical results.

As shown above, biased technological progress with the elasticity of substitution σ above 1 cannot explain the observed trends of the main macro variables. In the following discussions, we assume that σ is below unity.

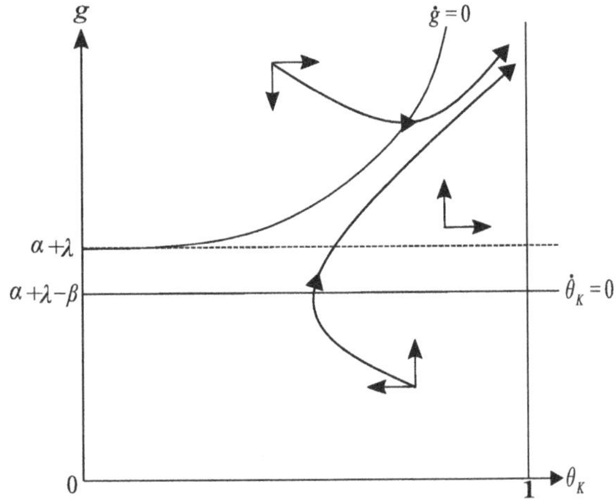

Fig. 1.3 Dynamics of θ_K and g under labor-saving technological progress ($\beta > 0$, $\sigma > 1$)

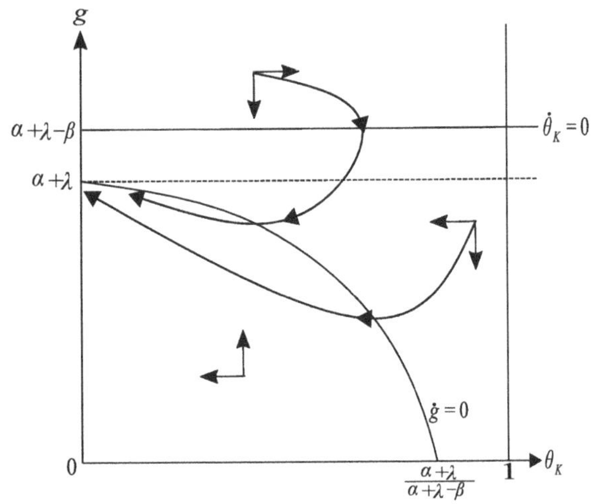

Fig. 1.4 Dynamics of θ_K and g under capital-saving technological progress ($\beta < 0$, $\sigma > 1$)

1.5 Conditions for the Introduction of Biased Technology and Its Direct Effects

1.5.1 Conditions for the Introduction of Biased Technology

We have so far assumed that whether technological progress becomes neutral, labor-saving or capital-saving is determined exogenously. In this section, we attempt to explain the introduction of biased technological progress as the choice of firms. We below find the conditions under which firms have incentives to introduce labor-saving or capital-saving technological progress.

Let us assume that the economy is initially at the steady state equilibrium under neutral technological progress ($\alpha \equiv \dot{A}/A > 0$ and $\beta \equiv \dot{\beta}/B = 0$). In this case, the capital/labor ratio measured in efficiency units $k^* \equiv (BK/AN)^*$ is constant, and since B is constant, $(K/AN)^*$ is also constant. Assuming this situation, let us examine whether firms have any incentive to introduce capital-saving ($\Delta B/B > 0$ under $\sigma < 1$) or labor-saving technologies ($\Delta B/B < 0$ under $\sigma < 1$). The question of whether firms will introduce such technology depends on whether it is profitable for them to do so, which amounts to the question of whether doing so raises the rate of return on capital r. The direct effects of a change in B on the rate of return on capital r is calculated from Eq. (1.9) and the definition of $k \equiv BK/AN$ as follows:

$$\frac{\Delta r}{\Delta B} = f'(k) + Bf''(k)\frac{\Delta k}{\Delta B} = f'(k)\left(1 - \frac{1 - \theta_K}{\sigma}\right), \tag{1.28}$$

where θ_K is the capital share of income defined by (1.11) and, therefore, $1 - \theta_K$ is the labor share of income (wages). σ is the elasticity of substitution between labor and capital defined by (1.14). From (1.28), we have the following result:

$$\text{If } 1 - \theta_K > \sigma, \text{ then } \Delta r/\Delta B < 0, \quad \text{if } 1 - \theta_K < 0, \text{ then } \Delta r/\Delta B > 0. \tag{1.29}$$

This result implies that if the labor share of income exceeds the elasticity of substitution between labor and capital ($1 - \theta_K > \sigma$), the introduction of labor-saving technology ($\Delta B < 0$) raises the rate of return on capital ($\Delta r > 0$), which is profitable for firms. In the opposite case ($1 - \theta_K < \sigma$), the introduction of capital-saving technology ($\Delta B > 0$) is profitable for firms ($\Delta r > 0$). Only if the labor share of income is equal to the elasticity of substitution between labor and capital ($1 - \theta_K = \sigma$), maintaining neutral technological progress ($\Delta B = 0$) is optimal for firms.

The above results may be summarized by the following proposition.

Proposition 1.4 *Assume that the economy is initially at the steady state equilibrium under neutral technological progress with a constant rate α. In this case, if firms choose the type of technological progress that increases the rate of return on capital as much as possible, the type of technology introduced by firms depends on the value of the labor share of income $1 - \theta_K$ relative to that of the elasticity of substitution between labor and capital σ as follows:*

(1) If $1 - \theta_K > \sigma$, labor-saving technology ($\Delta B < 0$) is introduced.
(2) If $1 - \theta_K < \sigma < 1$, capital-saving technology ($\Delta B > 0$) is introduced.
(3) If $1 - \theta_K = \sigma$, neutral technological progress ($\Delta B = 0$) is maintained.

This proposition implies that at any steady state equilibrium under neutral technological progress, this achieved neutral technological progress may not be optimal from the standpoint of firms. Namely, depending on the value of the labor share of income relative to the elasticity of substitution, there may be cases where introducing biased technology is more profitable for firms. The result of Proposition 1.4 may be formulated as a function explaining the rate of capital-augmenting technological progress $\Delta B/B \equiv \beta$ as follows:

$$\frac{\Delta B}{B} = \beta(1-\theta_K-\sigma), \quad \beta(0)=0, \quad \beta' < 0, \tag{1.30}$$

where the labor-augmenting technological progress rate $\alpha \equiv \Delta A/A$ is assumed to be constant.

1.5.2 Direct Effects of the Introduction of Biased Technology

Let us now examine the effects of the introduction of biased technology on the main macro variables, such as the capital share of income θ_K, the capital/output ratio K/Y, and the wage rate w/A. Considering the definition $k \equiv BK/AN$, and calculating from (1.6), (1.11), (1.12), and (1.10), we have the following results concerning the direct effects of introducing biased technological progress:

$$\frac{\Delta g}{g} = \theta_K \frac{\Delta B}{B} = \theta_K \beta(1-\theta_K-\sigma), \tag{1.31a}$$

$$\frac{\Delta \theta_K}{\theta_K} = \frac{\sigma-1}{\sigma}\frac{\Delta B}{B} = \frac{\sigma-1}{\sigma}\beta(1-\theta_K-\sigma), \tag{1.31b}$$

$$\frac{\Delta(K/Y)}{K/Y} = -\theta_K \frac{\Delta B}{B} = -\theta_K \beta(1-\theta_K-\sigma), \tag{1.31c}$$

$$\frac{\Delta(w/A)}{w/A} = \frac{1-\theta_K}{\sigma}\frac{\Delta B}{B} = \frac{1-\theta_K}{\sigma}\beta(1-\theta_K-\sigma), \tag{1.31d}$$

where Eq. (1.30) is taken into consideration. These equations mean the following: if $1-\theta_K > \sigma$, then $\Delta B/B < 0$ (labor-saving technological progress occurs), and therefore $\Delta g < 0$ (the growth rate of capital stock falls), $\Delta\theta_K > 0$ (the capital share of income rises), $\Delta(K/Y) > 0$ (the capital/output ratio rises), and $\Delta(w/A) < 0$ (the wage rate in the efficiency unit falls). If $1-\theta_K < \sigma < 1$, then $\Delta B/B > 0$ (capital-saving technological progress occurs), which has the opposite effects on those variables. Finally, if $1-\theta_K = \sigma$, then $\Delta B/B = 0$ (neutral technological progress is maintained), so that the capital share of income θ_K, the capital/output rate K/Y, and the wage rate in the efficiency unit w/A remain unchanged.

The above results may be summarized by the following proposition.

Proposition 1.5 *When firms introduce the type of technology based on the criterion mentioned in Proposition 4, the direct effects of the introduced technology on the main macro variables are as follows:*

(1) If the labor share of income is greater than the elasticity of substitution between labor and capital ($1-\theta_K > \sigma$), labor-saving technology is introduced ($\Delta B/B < 0$) and, as a result, the growth rate of capital stock (g) falls, the capital share

of income (θ_K) rises, the capital/output rate (K/Y) rises, and the wage rate measured in efficiency units (w/A) falls.

(2) *If the labor share of income is less than the elasticity of substitution between labor and capital ($1 - \theta_K < \sigma < 1$), capital-saving technology is introduced ($\Delta B/B > 0$) and, as a result, the growth rate of capital stock (g) rises, the capital share of income (θ_K) falls, the capital/output rate (K/Y) falls, and the wage rate (w/A) measured in efficiency units rises.*

(3) *When the labor share of income is equal to the elasticity of substitution between labor and capital ($1 - \theta_K = \sigma$), neutral technological progress is maintained ($\Delta B/B = 0$) and, as a result, the growth rate of capital stock, the capital share of income (θ_K), the capital/output rate (K/Y), and the wage rate (w/A) measured by efficiency units remain unchanged.*

As this proposition shows, if $1-\theta_K > \sigma$, the labor share of income $1-\theta_K$ decreases due to labor-saving technological progress, and conversely, if $1 - \theta_K < \sigma$, the labor share of income $1 - \theta_K$ increases due to capital-saving technological progress. In this way, the labor share of income $1 - \theta_K$ tends to be adjusted to the value of the elasticity of substitution σ in the long run, through firms' choices of the technology type.

In the above analysis, we assumed the rate of labor-augmenting technological progress ($\Delta A/A \equiv \alpha$) to be constant and focused on capital-augmenting technological progress ($\Delta B/B = \beta$), which causes bias in technology. We found that the effects of changes in B on the rate of return on capital can be either positive or negative. On the other hand, the effects of changes in A on the rate of return on capital are shown to be the following:

$$\frac{\Delta R}{\Delta A} = -\frac{B}{A}kf''(k) > 0.$$

Thus, an increase in A always raises the rate of return on capital, which implies that introducing labor-augmenting technology is always profitable for firms. However, if firms incur costs for technological innovation, it is not the case that a higher rate of labor-augmenting technological progress brings about a higher rate of return on capital. Particularly, if the resources for technological innovation are given, there may be a trade-off relationship between the rate of labor-augmenting technological progress α and the rate of capital-augmenting technological progress rate β.[20] In the next chapter, we develop a model that takes this trade-off into consideration.

[20]The trade-off relationship between the rate of labor-augmenting technological progress α and the rate of capital-augmenting technological progress β is called the innovation possibility frontier, and the growth model that incorporates this hypothesis is the induced invention model. We will develop that model in the next chapter.

1.6 Conclusions

Technological progress is considered to be the most important factor for improving social welfare, since it constantly increases per capita income over time. Therefore, the analysis of technological progress has been the core of growth theories. Those growth theories mostly deal with the case of neutral (labor-augmenting) technological progress, which enables achievement of the steady state equilibrium. The steady state equilibrium is regarded as important because it is consistent with the stylized facts of capitalist development. However, in his recent empirical studies, Piketty used long-term data of various major countries to examine long-term trends of the main macro variables, such as the capital/output ratio, capital share of income, and rate of return on capital, and found that those variables do not remain constant as the stylized facts of capitalist economy assert but have rising or falling trends even in the long run. To explain those empirical results theoretically, Piketty argues that the elasticity of substitution between labor and capital must be above 1. However, almost all empirical studies on the elasticity of substitution obtained results showing this value is below 1.

In this chapter, we investigated the role of biased technological progress in economic growth and income distribution, using the framework of the neoclassical growth model. We have shown that, if biased technological progress is taken into consideration, Piketty's empirical results are consistently explained even if the elasticity of substitution between labor and capital is below 1. Additionally, it was shown that if technological progress is labor-saving, the growth rate of productivity as well as that of the real wage rate tends to decline as the capital share of income rises. This result suggests that labor-saving technological progress may be one possible factor that explains the "productivity paradox" pointed out by Solow. We then investigated the conditions under which firms have incentives to introduce labor-saving (or capital-saving) technological progress. We found that if firms choose a technology type that increases the rate of return on capital, labor-saving (or capital-saving) technological progress is introduced when the labor share of income exceeds (or falls short of) the elasticity of substitution between labor and capital. Moreover, it was shown that the introduction of labor-saving (or capital-saving) technological progress lowers (or raises) the labor share of income and, as a result, the labor share of income is adjusted towards the value of the elasticity of substitution between labor and capital. In this analysis, we assumed that firms choose the optimal rate of capital-augmenting technological progress with the rate of labor-augmenting technological progress remaining constant. However, if we assume that the resources for technological innovation are given, there may be a trade-off relationship between the rate of labor-augmenting technological progress and the rate of capital-augmenting technological progress. This case will be examined in the next chapter.

Chapter 2
Growth and Income Distribution Under Induced Innovation

Abstract To explain the long-run fluctuations of growth and income distribution consistent with the data shown in Piketty (Capital in the twenty-first century. Belknap Press of Harvard University Press, Cambridge, 2014), two types of technological progress, labor-saving and capital-saving, must alternately emerge. With a modification of induced innovation theory, this chapter first analyzes the firm's choice of type of technological progress based on the present value maximization criterion. Incorporating endogenous type choice into the standard neoclassical growth model, we next examine the long-run dynamics of the macroeconomy. Assuming that the innovation possibility frontier, the key concept in induced innovation theory, shifts up or down depending on the rate of capital accumulation, we modify the model so that it is capable of explaining the aforementioned alternating emergence. Finally, we derive the socially optimal type of innovation to compare it with the market outcome. As a result, it is shown that the innovation attained by the market is not socially optimal. This implies that policies in the capital markets such as taxation and possibly regulation are necessary.

Keywords Innovation possibility frontier · Present value maximization
Elasticity of substitution between labor and capital · Capital share of income
Capital/output ratio

2.1 Introduction

This chapter investigates the theory of induced innovation that endogenizes a firm's type of technological progress and analyzes the long-run fluctuations of growth and income distribution based on that theory. The long-run data in Piketty (2014) has made it clear that the phase in which both the capital share of income and the capital-output ratio increase persists, and then the phase in which they both decrease alternately persists. To explain this fact based on the model in the previous chapter, labor-saving technological progress and capital-saving technological progress must emerge alternately. Induced innovation theory rigorously analyzes the choice of the

H. Adachi et al., *Technological Progress, Income Distribution, and Unemployment*,
Kobe University Social Science Research Series,
https://doi.org/10.1007/978-981-13-3726-0_2

type of technological progress and the alternation of the choices. The theory explains how growth and income distribution evolve through changes in types of technological progress when the firm chooses technology that maximizes the reduction in production costs under the constraint of an *innovation possibility frontier*, which demonstrates a tradeoff between the rate of labor-augmenting technological progress α and the rate of capital-augmenting technological progress β.[1]

Two important purposes of this chapter are to point out two drawbacks in the basic theory of induced innovation and develop a model that overcomes them. The first drawback lies in the assumption that the firm determines technological progress so as to maximize *the rate of reduction in current period costs*. This assumption is equivalent to maximization of the output growth rate. However, it is not plausible to assume this objective function for technology choice from the viewpoint of consistency because profit maximization is assumed in determining the firm's factor demands. A more natural formulation, similar to decisions on factor demands, is to assume that the firm chooses technology so as to maximize the present value of profits under the constraint of an innovation possibility frontier.[2] Based on the formulation, this chapter analyzes the firm's technology choice. As a result, it is shown that the elasticity of substitution between labor and capital plays a crucial role in the choice of a type of technological progress. Also, suppose that the type of innovation that maximizes output is the socially optimal one. We can then compare the type of innovation under the present value maximization criterion with the socially optimal type of innovation.

The second drawback is related to *innovation possibility frontiers*. An innovation possibility frontier represents the tradeoff where an increase in the rate of labor-augmenting technological progress α entails costs of a decrease in the rate of capital-augmenting technological progress β, which is shown by a downward-sloping curve in the (α, β) plane.[3] The type of innovation is chosen as a point on the curve that maximizes the present value of the firm, and income distribution is determined accordingly. Thus, the curve plays a crucial role in determining income distribution. It is noteworthy that the tradeoff between labor-augmenting technological progress and capital-augmenting technological progress is derived implicitly, assuming resources usable for innovation are given. It is therefore plausible to assume that if resources change, the frontier is shifted upward or downward accordingly.[4] Introducing a variable that influences resources, we consider the possibility of a shift of the innovation possibility frontier. This chapter overcomes these two drawbacks to develop a modified version of induced innovation.

---

[1]This chapter is based on a large literature of factor-biased innovation, going back to Kennedy (1964), Drandakis and Phelps (1966), Samuelson (1966), and Ahmad (1966). It is also based on the recent revival by Acemoglu (2010) and Stiglitz (2014), among others.

[2]Acemoglu (2003) also develops the same argument.

[3]See Fig. 2.1 in Sect. 2.2.

[4]Nordhaus (1973) criticizes the stationary nature of the innovation possibility frontier as unrealistic. The model we develop in this chapter provides a simple solution to this problem, although it may not fully cope with his criticism.

The rest of this chapter is organized as follows. In Sect. 2.2, we examine the decisions of the firm on employment, investment, and technology based on present value maximization of profits, especially focusing on the determination of the type of technological progress. In Sect. 2.3, we present a model of induced innovation incorporating the firm's decision on technology derived in Sect. 2.2, and examine the long-run dynamics. Section 2.4 extends the model to one where the rate of capital accumulation influences the innovation possibility frontier, causing it to shift. This model is shown to be able to explain the empirical findings in Piketty (2014). Section 2.5 compares the innovation type under the firm's present value maximization with that of the social optimum and refers to its implication for income distribution. Section 2.6 concludes this chapter.

2.2 Decisions on Employment, Investment and Technology

As mentioned before, the existing theory of induced innovation assumes that the type of technological progress is determined so as to maximize the rate of cost reduction at a given factor ratio. However, the maximization is not a natural way to formulate the firm's motivation, as noted in the introduction. Based on the present-value maximization of the firm, this section examines decisions on employment, investment, and technology.

The production function is homogenous of degree one and takes the following form:

$$Y = F(AN, BK), \tag{2.1}$$

where Y is output, N is labor, K is capital stock, A is the labor efficiency parameter, and B is the capital efficiency parameter. Since the function is linearly homogenous, it can be rewritten as follows:

$$\frac{Y}{AN} = f\left(\frac{B}{A}\tilde{k}\right) = f(k), \tag{2.2}$$

where $f(\cdot)$ is a function representing output per efficiency unit of labor, $\tilde{k} = K/L$ is the capital-labor ratio, and $k = BK/AL$ is the capital-labor ratio in efficiency units.

As shown in Fig. 2.1, a tradeoff is assumed to exist between labor-augmenting technological progress, that is $\Delta A/A \equiv \alpha$, and capital-augmenting technological progress, $\Delta B/B \equiv \beta$. The tradeoff is the innovation possibility frontier, which was first proposed by Kennedy (1964), and can be expressed as the following function:

$$\beta = \beta(\alpha) \quad \text{where} \quad \beta'(\alpha) < 0 \quad \text{and} \quad \beta''(\alpha) < 0. \tag{2.3}$$

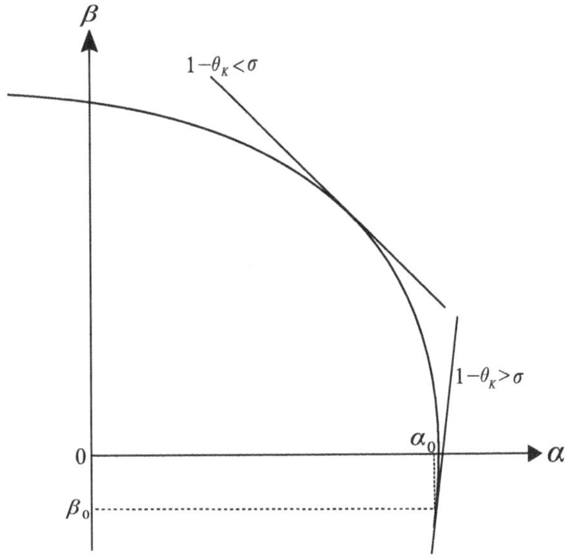

Fig. 2.1 Innovation possibility frontier

The rate of labor-augmenting technological progress α can be increased at the expense of a decline in capital-augmenting technological progress β. In addition, the decline in β accelerates as α increases.

The firm is assumed to maximize the discounted sum of profits over two periods, and hence the objective function is given by:

$$V = F(A_0 N_0, B_0 K_0) - W_0 N_0 - I_0 + \frac{1}{1+r}\{F(A_1 N_1, B_1 K_1) - W_1 N_1 + K_1\}, \quad (2.4)$$

where W is the wage rate per labor input, r is the interest rate, and I is investment. A subscript 0 represents the current period, while 1 represents the next period. The state variables must satisfy the following relationships:

$$K_1 = K_0 + I_0, \quad N_1 = N_0(1+\lambda), \quad A_1 = A_0(1+\alpha), \quad B_1 = B_0(1+\beta) \quad (2.5)$$

where λ stands for the growth rate of labor. The first-order condition for labor input N_t is

$$A_t F_{Nt} = W_t \quad \text{for} \quad t = 0, 1 \quad (2.6)$$

and for investment I_0 is

$$B_1 F_{K1} = r. \quad (2.7)$$

With wage rates W_0, W_1, and the interest rate r given, the firm determines employment each period so as to equate the marginal product of labor with the same period's wage rate (2.6), and investment so as to equate the marginal product of capital with the given interest rate (2.7).

Next, let us analyze the choice of technological progress type by the firm. From (2.1) and (2.2), the production function per efficiency unit can be expressed as the following:

$$F(A_tN_t, B_tK_t) = f((B_t/K_t)\tilde{k}_t)A_tN_t \quad \text{for } t = 0, 1. \tag{2.8}$$

Using the above, (2.6), which represents equalization of the marginal product of labor with the wage rate, becomes

$$W_t = A_t\left\{f\left(\frac{B_t}{A_t}\tilde{k}_t\right) - \frac{B_t}{A_t}\tilde{k}_t f'\left(\frac{B_t}{A_t}\tilde{k}_t\right)\right\} \quad \text{for } t = 0, 1. \tag{2.9}$$

Substituting (2.8) and (2.9) into (2.4) gives

$$V = B_0 f'\left(\frac{B_0}{A_0}\tilde{k}_0\right)K_0 - I_0 + \frac{1}{1+r}\left\{B_1 f'\left(\frac{B_1}{A_1}\tilde{k}_1\right)K_1 + K_1\right\}, \tag{2.10}$$

where

$$A_1 = A_0(1+\alpha), \quad B_1 = B_0(1+\beta). \tag{2.11}$$

The firm's decision regarding choice of technological progress type therefore becomes the problem of maximizing the present value, given by (2.10), subject to the innovation possibility frontier, given by (2.3). For the firm to maximize (2.10), it simply maximizes the next period's marginal product of capital, in other words, $B_1 f'((B_1/A_1)\tilde{k}_1)$. Taking (2.3) and (2.11) into account, the marginal product of capital at period 0, $M(\alpha)$, becomes:

$$M(\alpha) = B_0(1+\beta(\alpha))f'\left(\frac{B_0(1+\beta(\alpha))}{A_0(1+\alpha)}\tilde{k}_1\right). \tag{2.12}$$

$M(\alpha)$ is maximized at α^* that satisfies $M'(\alpha^*) = 0$. Taking the log-derivative of (2.12),

$$\frac{M'(\alpha)}{M(\alpha)} = \frac{\beta'(\alpha)}{1+\beta(\alpha)} - \frac{1-\theta_K(k_1)}{\sigma}\left(\frac{\beta'(\alpha)}{1+\beta(\alpha)} - \frac{1}{1+\alpha}\right), \tag{2.13}$$

where θ_K is the capital elasticity of output and σ is the elasticity of substitution between labor and capital, which are defined as follows:

$$\theta_K(k_1) \equiv \frac{k_1 f'(k_1)}{f(k_1)} \quad \text{where } k_1 \equiv \frac{B_1K_1}{A_1N_1} = \frac{B_0(1+\beta(\alpha))}{A_0(1+\alpha)}\tilde{k}_1, \tag{2.14}$$

$$\sigma \equiv -\frac{f'(k_1)\{f(k_1) - k_1 f'(k_1)\}}{k_1 f''(k_1) f(k_1)}. \tag{2.15}$$

θ_K is a function of k_1, and is equal to the capital share of income under perfect competition, and hence $0 < \theta_K < 1$. Although σ is in general a function of k_1, to simplify the argument, it is assumed to be constant. In other words, the production function is assumed to be of CES type.

Rewriting (2.13),

$$\frac{M'(\alpha)}{M(\alpha)} = \frac{1 - \theta_K(k_1) - G(\alpha)\{1 - \theta_K(k_1) - \sigma\}}{(1+\alpha)\sigma} \quad \text{where} \quad G(\alpha) \equiv \frac{(1+\alpha)\beta'(\alpha)}{1+\beta(\alpha)}. \tag{2.16}$$

From the property of the innovation possibility frontier (2.3), we have

$$G(\alpha) < 0 \quad \text{and} \quad G'(\alpha) < 0. \tag{2.17}$$

Therefore, α^* that satisfies $M'(\alpha^*) = 0$ can be obtained as the solution to the following equation:

$$G(\alpha^*) = \frac{1 - \theta_K(k_1)}{1 - \theta_K(k_1) - \sigma} = \frac{1 - \theta_K\left(\{B_0(1+\beta(\alpha^*))/A_0(1+\alpha^*)\}\tilde{k}_1\right)}{1 - \theta_K\left(\{B_0(1+\beta(\alpha^*))/A_0(1+\alpha^*)\}\tilde{k}_1\right) - \sigma}. \tag{2.18}$$

Thus, given $\tilde{k}_1$, the optimal type of technological progress is determined by this equation. Since $G(\alpha) < 0$ and $0 < \theta_K < 1$, the equation has a solution if and only if $1 - \theta_K < \sigma$.

Let us briefly discuss the case that $1 - \theta_K \geq \sigma$. Since, as evident from (2.16), $M'(\alpha) > 0$ holds for any possible α in this case, it is optimal to increase α as much as possible. The maximum possible value of α is achieved at the corner of the innovation possibility frontier. Denoting the value as α_0, the optimal solution is α_0. The rate of capital-augmenting technological progress corresponding to α_0 is $\beta_0 = \beta(\alpha_0) < 0$.[5] This implies that the optimal type of technological change is labor-saving. As long as the inequality $1 - \theta_K \geq \sigma$ holds, labor-saving technological progress is always chosen.

The above findings can be summarized as the following proposition.

Proposition 2.1 *Suppose that the firm determines the type of technological progress under the innovation possibility frontier $\beta = \beta(\alpha)$. Then, if $1 - \theta_K < \sigma$, the rate of labor-augmenting technological progress α^* and the corresponding rate of capital-augmenting technological progress β^* satisfying (2.18) are the optimal types of technological progress for the firm. If, instead, $1 - \theta_K \geq \sigma$, then the corner solution $(\alpha_0, \beta(\alpha_0))$, at which the rate of labor-augmenting technological progress on the innovation possibility frontier takes the maximum possible value, is optimal. Since*

---

[5] See Fig. 2.1.

the solution also maximizes the present value, it is optimal for the firm. The rate of capital-augmenting technological progress at the solution is $\beta_0 = \beta(\alpha_0) < 0$*, and hence the optimal type of technological progress is labor-saving.*

2.3 Long-Run Dynamics and Biased Technological Progress

In the previous section, we discussed the firm's determination of employment, investment, and technological progress. In this section, based on the analysis in the previous section, we analyze the dynamics of the economy as a whole, incorporating capital accumulation into the model. Although a two-period model in discrete time is employed in the previous section to clarify the decision process, we use the continuous-time model in the following analysis.

2.3.1 *The Model of Long-Run Dynamics*

Assuming a constant share of income s is saved and invested, capital accumulation is expressed as follows:

$$\dot{K} = I = sY, \tag{2.19}$$

where I is physical investment, and a dot over a variable (x) stands for its time-derivative ($\dot{x} \equiv dx/dt$). Substituting the production function (2.2) into (2.19), we have

$$\frac{\dot{K}}{K} = s\frac{Y}{K} = s\frac{Bf(k)}{k}. \tag{2.20}$$

Let us introduce the continuous-time version of the aforementioned innovation possibility frontier. Suppose that $\alpha \equiv \dot{A}/A$ is the rate of labor-augmenting technological progress and $\beta \equiv \dot{B}/B$ is the rate of capital-augmenting technological progress. Then, the frontier can be expressed as the following function:

$$\frac{\dot{B}}{B} = \beta\left(\frac{\dot{A}}{A}\right) \quad \text{or} \quad \beta = \beta(\alpha) \quad \text{where} \quad \beta' < 0, \quad \beta'' < 0. \tag{2.21}$$

Let us examine how the optimal decisions of the firm regarding employment, investment and technological progress are formulated for the continuous-time case. The firm's objective function at present time t over a future period $t + h$ is given by

$$V = \int_{t}^{t+h} \{F(A_\tau N_\tau, B_\tau K_\tau) - W_\tau N_\tau - I_\tau\} e^{-r(\tau - t)} d\tau + K_{t+h}, \tag{2.22}$$

where K_{t+h} is a given terminal capital stock. Then, the maximizing condition for employment is given by (2.6), which amounts to (2.9), holding at each point of time in the interval $[t, t + h]$. As for investment, we assume it to be determined to maximize (2.22) subject to (2.19), adopting the neoclassical theory of investment due to Jorgenson.[6] In this case, the optimal capital stock at time t, denoted by K^*_{t+h}, is determined at the level that equalizes the marginal productivity of capital to the rate of interest:

$$r = B_t F_K(A_t N_t, B_t K_t^*). \tag{2.23}$$

Then, investment at time t is determined by

$$I_t = \delta(K_t^* - K_t), \tag{2.24}$$

where K_t is actual capital stock at time t and δ is a parameter representing the speed of adjustment. Thus, investment at time t depends on the state of technology (A_t, B_t) employment (N_t), capital stock (K_t) and the rate of interest (r) at that time.

Assuming that the optimal decisions on employment and investment have thus been made, we next consider the optimal behavior for technological progress in continuous time. Substituting (2.8) and (2.9) for $[t, t+h]$ into (2.22), we can rewrite the firm's objective function as follows:

$$V = \int_{t}^{t+h} M_\tau K_\tau e^{-r(\tau - t)} d\tau - \int_{t}^{t+h} I_\tau e^{-r(\tau - t)} d\tau + K_{t+h}, \tag{2.25}$$

where

$$M_\tau = B_\tau f'(k_\tau) = B_\tau f'\left(\frac{B_\tau}{A_\tau} \tilde{k}_\tau\right). \tag{2.26}$$

When we discuss about the optimal decision on technological progress, we may concentrate on the maximization of the first term on the right-hand side of (2.25), since investment has already been determined optimally as discussed above. In other words, the firm's decision regarding technological progress can be formulated as an optimization problem for determining α so as to maximize

[6] See, for example, Jorgenson (1963).

$$\tilde{V} = \int_{t}^{t+h} M_\tau K_\tau e^{-r(\tau - t)} d\tau, \tag{2.27}$$

subject to (2.21). However, this maximization can be shown to be equivalent to maximization of $\dot{M} \equiv dM/dt$.[7] From (2.21) and (2.26), under given $\tilde{k}_t$, $\dot{M} \equiv dM/dt$ becomes

$$\frac{\dot{M}}{M} = \left(1 - \frac{1-\theta_K(k)}{\sigma}\right)\frac{\dot{B}}{B} + \frac{1-\theta_K(k)}{\sigma}\frac{\dot{A}}{A} = \frac{1}{\sigma}[\{\sigma - 1 + \theta_K(k)\}\beta(\alpha) + \{1 - \theta_K(k)\}\alpha]. \tag{2.28}$$

The first-order condition for α is as follows:

$$\frac{\partial \dot{M}}{\partial \alpha} = \frac{M}{\sigma}[\{\sigma - 1 + \theta_K(k)\}\beta'(\alpha) + \{1 - \theta_K(k)\}] = 0, \tag{2.29}$$

and hence the optimal rate of labor-augmenting technological progress α must satisfy the following condition:

$$\beta'(\alpha^*) = \frac{1 - \theta_K(k)}{1 - \theta_K(k) - \sigma}. \tag{2.30}$$

Since $\beta'(\alpha) < 0$ and $0 < \theta_K < 1$, for the above to have a meaningful solution, $1 - \theta_K(k) < \sigma$ must hold. We will discuss the case that $1 - \theta_K(k) \geq \sigma$ later.

Assuming the condition for the existence of an interior solution, that is, $1-\theta_K(k) < \sigma$, α becomes a continuous and decreasing function of θ_K as follows:

$$\alpha = \phi(\theta_K)\, where \quad \phi' < 0. \tag{2.31}$$

In turn, θ_K is a function of k, and the derivative with respect to k has the following properties:

$$\theta_K'(k) = \theta_K(k)\{1 - \theta_K(k)\}\frac{\sigma - 1}{\sigma} \gtreqless 0 \quad \Leftrightarrow \quad \sigma \gtreqless 1. \tag{2.32}$$

From (2.31) and (2.32), α becomes the following function of k:

---

[7] See Mathematical Appendix for the proof.

$$\alpha = \alpha(k) \text{ and } \alpha'(k) \underset{<}{\overset{>}{=}} 0 \quad \Leftrightarrow \quad \sigma \underset{>}{\overset{<}{=}} 1 \tag{2.33}$$

Substituting the above into (2.21), the innovation possibility frontier becomes:

$$\frac{\dot{B}}{B} \equiv \beta = \beta(\alpha(k)). \tag{2.34}$$

As (2.34) shows, the direction of technological progress is uniquely determined according to a given k.

Differentiating the capital-labor ratio in terms of efficiency units $k \equiv BK/AN$ with respect to time, and then substituting (2.20), (2.33), and (2.34) into the result, we have the following differential equation:

$$\frac{\dot{k}}{k} = sB\frac{f(k)}{k} + \beta(\alpha(k)) - \alpha(k) - \lambda, \tag{2.35}$$

where λ is the growth rate of labor; in other words, $\lambda \equiv \dot{N}/N$ in continuous-time. Equations (2.34) and (2.35) constitute a complete dynamic system.

Let us turn to the case that $1 - \theta_K(k) \geq \sigma$. In this case, the maximand (2.27) has no interior solution for α. As stated in Proposition 1, the present value of the firm achieves its maximum when the rate of labor-augmenting technological progress α takes the maximum value on the innovation possibility frontier; that is, at the corner of the frontier $(\alpha_0, \beta(\alpha_0))$,[8] which is the optimal type of technological progress for the firm. The technological progress is labor-saving because $\beta(\alpha_0) < 0$. The dynamic system characterizing the economy consists of the following two differential equations:

$$\frac{\dot{B}}{B} = \beta(\alpha_0) < 0, \tag{2.36}$$

$$\frac{\dot{k}}{k} = sB\frac{f(k)}{k} + \beta(\alpha_0) - \alpha_0 - \lambda. \tag{2.37}$$

In what follows, we will examine the system consisting of (2.34) and (2.35) and that consisting of (2.36) and (2.37). Each system exhibits different dynamics depending on whether σ is smaller or larger than unity. Hence, let us analyze the case where $\sigma < 1$ first, and then the case where $\sigma > 1$.

---

[8]See Fig. 2.1.

2.3.2 Dynamics When $\sigma < 1$

When $\sigma < 1$, as is evident from (2.32), the capital share $\theta_K = \theta_K(k)$ is monotonically decreasing with k. Therefore, as long as σ is constant, $\bar{k}$ that satisfies $1 - \theta_K(\bar{k}) = \sigma$ uniquely exists. While $1 - \theta_K(k) < \sigma < 1$ if $k < \bar{k}$, $1 - \theta_K(k) \geq \sigma$ if $k \geq \bar{k}$. The dynamic system consisting of (2.34) and (2.35) emerges when $k < \bar{k}$, while the system of (2.36) and (2.37) emerges when $k \geq \bar{k}$.

First, let us examine the dynamics when $1 - \theta_K(k) < \sigma < 1$, or when the economy is in the realm of $k < \bar{k}$. It is therefore characterized by the system consisting of (2.34) and (2.35). The steady state is determined by the following system of equations:

$$\beta(\alpha(k^*)) = 0, \tag{2.38}$$

$$B^* = \frac{k^*}{sf(k^*)}[\lambda + \alpha(k^*)]. \tag{2.39}$$

Since $\alpha = \alpha(k)$ is a monotonically increasing function and $\beta = \beta(\alpha)$ is a monotonically decreasing function, $\beta = \beta(\alpha(k))$ is monotonically decreasing with k. Equation (2.38) therefore has a unique solution of k^*. Once k^* is given, B^* is uniquely determined by (2.39).

As shown in Fig. 2.2, the locus of $\dot{B} = 0$ is a vertical line in the (k, B) plane. By assumption, $k^* < \bar{k}$ must hold. From (2.35), the locus of $\dot{k} = 0$ in the (k, B) plane is depicted as an upward-sloping curve in the realm of $k < \bar{k}$. Turning to the law of motion, B decreases in the region right of the locus of $\dot{B} = 0$, while it increases in the opposite region. As Fig. 2.2 shows, therefore the system characterized by (k, B) gradually converges to the steady state equilibrium with cyclical behavior.

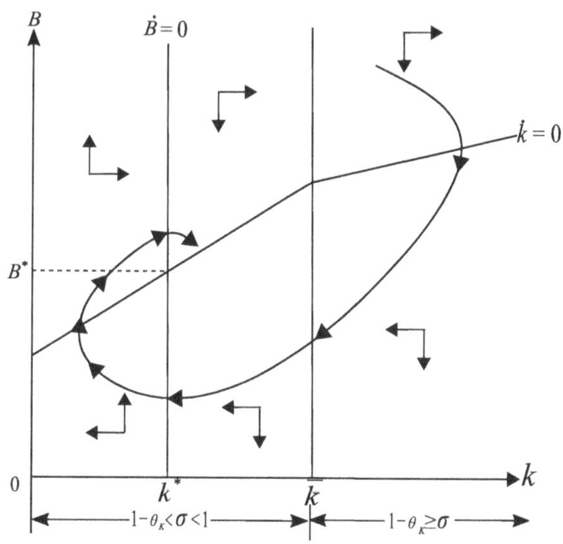

Fig. 2.2 Phase diagram when $\sigma < 1$

Next, let us examine the dynamics when $1 - \theta_K(k) \geq \sigma$, or when the economy is in the realm of $k \geq \bar{k}$. The upward-sloping curve in Fig. 2.2 shows the locus of $\dot{k} = 0$ in (2.33), which is the following relationship:

$$B = \frac{k}{sf(k)}[\alpha_0 + \lambda - \beta(\alpha_0)]. \tag{2.40}$$

Since the law of motion for B is determined by (2.36) in this region, as shown in Fig. 2.2, B continues to fall. In contrast, k increases above the curve of (2.40) but decreases below it. Hence, if the economy starts in the area above the locus of (2.40), k will surely enter the phase of declining, although it may initially increase for a while. When k decreases, the capital share of income θ_K increases, and hence the labor share $1-\theta_K$ decreases. Therefore, in the region of $k \geq \bar{k}$, the labor share $1-\theta_K$ continues to decrease under labor-saving technological progress ($\dot{B}/B < 0$). After this process continues for a certain period, $1 - \theta_K$ will surely become smaller than σ; that is, $1 - \theta_K < \sigma$, and hence the economy enters the region of $k < \bar{k}$. Since the dynamic system consisting of (2.34) and (2.35) emerges in this region, the economy finally converges to the steady state determined by (2.38) and (2.39).

2.3.3 Dynamics When $\sigma > 1$

When $\sigma > 1$, the dynamic system is now governed by (2.34) and (2.35), and hence the steady state equilibrium is given by (2.38) and (2.39). It should also be noted that $\alpha = \alpha(k)$ is a decreasing function when $\sigma > 1$, while it is an increasing function when $\sigma < 1$. As the phase diagram depicted in Fig. 2.3 shows, the steady state equilibrium has saddle-point stability. If the economy starts in the region above the saddle path converging to the steady state equilibrium (k^*, B^*), the firm chooses capital-saving technological progress ($\dot{B}/B > 0$) because the capital share of income is higher than the desirable level. This in turn further increases k, the capital-labor ratio in efficiency units, and hence k and B keep increasing. As a result, both diverge to infinity. In contrast, if the economy starts in the region below the saddle path, then labor-saving technological progress ($\dot{B}/B < 0$) is chosen because the capital share of income is lower than the desirable level. Since k and B keep decreasing, both move toward zero.

The above facts lead to the following proposition.

Proposition 2.2 *Suppose that the type of technological progress is endogenously determined by the firm to maximize the present value subject to the innovation possibility frontier. Then, the dynamic stability of the economy depends on the elasticity of substitution between capital and labor σ. If $\sigma < 1$, then the steady state equilibrium is stable, and hence the economy converges to it. If $\sigma > 1$, then the equilibrium is unstable, and hence the economy diverges from it.*

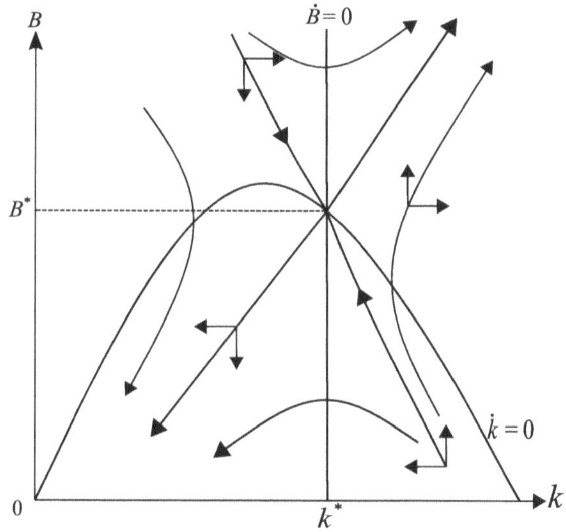

Fig. 2.3 Phase diagram when $\sigma > 1$

For clear understanding, let us summarize the detailed dynamic properties in the case that $\sigma < 1$ as the following proposition.

Proposition 2.3 *Suppose that $\sigma < 1$. Then, there exists $\bar{k}$ such that $1 - \theta_K(\bar{k}) = \sigma$. While $1 - \theta_K(k) < \sigma$ in the region that $k < \bar{k}$, $1 - \theta_K(k) \geq \sigma$ in the region that $k \geq \bar{k}$. The dynamics for each region are as follows:*

(1) *If the economy is in the region where $k < \bar{k}$, and hence $1 - \theta_K(k) < \sigma$, then there exists a unique steady state equilibrium determined by* (2.38) *and* (2.39). *The economy converges to the equilibrium either monotonically or cyclically.*
(2) *If the economy is in the region where $k \geq \bar{k}$, and hence $1 - \theta_K(k) \geq \sigma$, then the labor share of income $1 - \theta_K(k)$ decreases almost everywhere because the type of technological progress is always labor-saving ($\dot{B}/B < 0$). Since $1 - \theta_K(k) < \sigma$ will sooner or later be the case, the economy will enter the region where $k < \bar{k}$, and hence will converge in the long run to the steady state equilibrium determined by* (2.38) *and* (2.39).

2.3.4 The Effects of Population Growth and Saving Rates

Using the model presented in this chapter, let us examine the effects of a decline in population growth λ on technological progress, income distribution, and economic growth. Evidently from (2.34) and (2.35), a decline in λ has no impact on the $\dot{B} = 0$ locus but shifts the $\dot{k} = 0$ locus downward. Suppose that the economy is initially at the steady state P_0 in Fig. 2.4. As the result of a decline in population growth, the new steady state equilibrium moves to P_1, and the economy traces $P_0 \rightarrow Q \rightarrow R \rightarrow$

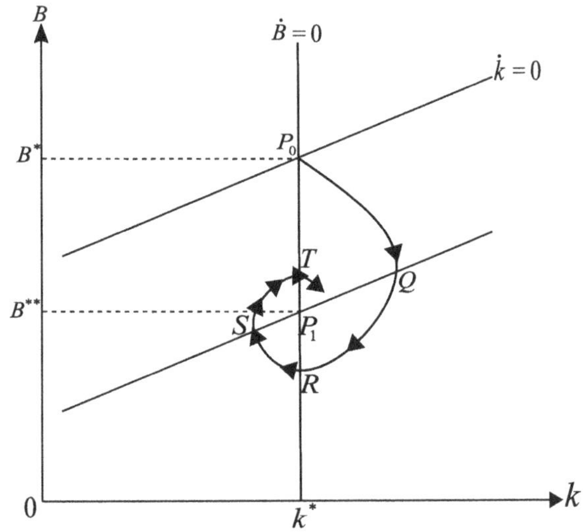

Fig. 2.4 Transitional dynamics after a decline in population growth

$S \rightarrow T$ during the transition to P_1. In the early phase of the transition ($P_0 \rightarrow Q$), B declines and k rises. When $\sigma < 1$, a rise in k lowers the capital share of income θ_K. Thus, since a decline in population growth decreases labor supply, it facilitates the introduction of labor-saving technological progress.

In the early phase, however, the capital share of income decreases because the effect of a wage increase due to the decline in labor supply is larger than that of the wage decrease due to the introduction of labor-saving technological progress. During the transition of $Q \rightarrow R$, B still decreases, but k enters a decreasing phase from the previously decreasing one. The effect of a wage decrease due to labor-saving technological progress becomes so effective that it raises the capital share of income θ_K. After this phase, the economy moves to the phase depicted by $R \rightarrow S$, where k continues to fall, while B begins to increase after k becomes smaller than k^*. This is because capital-saving technological progress becomes desirable for the firm. Although the capital share of income θ_K is still on the rise during this phase, the economy enters the phase depicted by $S \rightarrow T$, where θ_K starts to decline, after capital-saving technological progress is in effect. The above observations constitute the cyclical behavior of the economy converging to the steady state equilibrium. Thus, the type of technological progress changes from labor-saving to capital-saving. However, labor-saving technological progress is dominant during the transition to the new steady state. Although the capital share of income θ_K returns to the initial value, both capital stock and income growth decrease, and the capital-output ratio increases.

Next, let us examine the effects of the saving rate s. Suppose that s increases. Then, as Fig. 2.5 shows, the $\dot{B} = 0$ locus does not change, while the $\dot{k} = 0$ locus shifts upward. Capital-saving technological progress takes place during most of the transition converging to the new steady state. While the capital-output ratio is lower

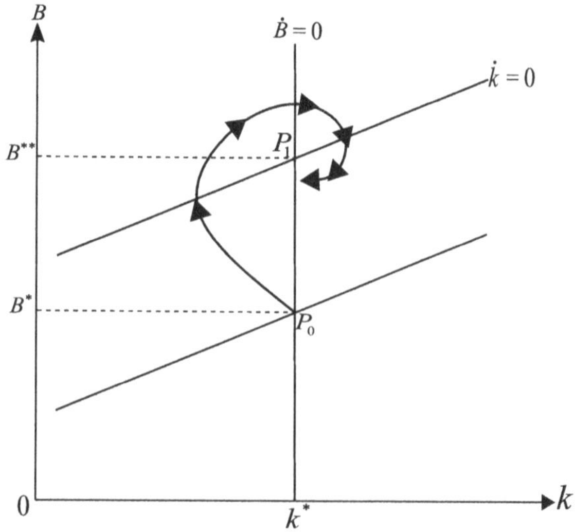

Fig. 2.5 Transitional dynamics after a decline in the saving rate

at the new steady state than at the initial one, the growth rate of capital stock (and of income) and the capital share of income do not change.

Let us summarize the above as the following proposition.

Proposition 2.4 *Suppose that a decline in population happens to an economy that is initially at the steady state equilibrium. Then, technological progress is labor-saving during most of the transition converging to the new steady state. Comparing the new steady state equilibrium with the initial one, while the capital-output ratio increases, the capital share of income does not change. When the saving rate falls, then capital-saving technological progress prevails during the transition. Comparing the new steady state equilibrium with the initial one, while the capital-output ratio decreases, the growth rate of capital stock (and of income) and the capital share of income do not change.*

In the model of induced innovation presented in this chapter, the economy converges to the steady state equilibrium when $\sigma < 1$. Since technological progress is neutral at the steady state equilibrium, the type of technological progress converges to the point $(\alpha^{*}, 0)$ on the innovation possibility frontier. The income share there stays constant as long as the possibility frontier is unchanged. The long-run data in Piketty (2014) introduced in Chap. 1 shows that the capital-output ratio and capital share of income increase in the phase in which the growth rates of capital stock and output decrease.[9] The model presented in this section does not account for an increase in the capital share of income. However, the next section develops a model to explain this.

[9]See Sect. 1.2 in Chap. 1.

2.4 Interactions Between Innovation and Capital Accumulation

2.4.1 *Investment and Technological Progress*

The model of induced innovation explains the direction of technological progress assuming the innovation possibility frontier that shows the tradeoff between labor-augmenting technological progress and capital-augmenting technological progress. Unlike the endogenous growth models, however, it is unable to explain the speed of technological progress. The innovation possibility frontier is depicted based on the assumption that an increase in labor-augmenting technological progress is only possible by decreasing capital-augmenting technological progress, and vice versa. Behind this tradeoff relationship, there is an implicit assumption that the resource usable for innovation is constant. It is plausible to consider that the frontier shifts if the resource changes. Constructing a model that incorporates possible shifts in the frontier, this section develops the model of induced innovation.

Firms' innovation is realized via their research and development (R&D) investment. Taking into account that the economy's investment as a whole consists of R&D investment in addition to physical capital investment, innovation itself is considered closely related to the total investment in the economy. Here, to simplify the analysis, assuming that a constant share δ of total investment is devoted to R&D investment, the growth rate of capital stock I/K is equal to that of R&D related or knowledge capital $\delta I/\delta K$. Introducing this growth variable $g \equiv I/K$ into the innovation possibility frontier as an additional argument, let us reformulate (2.21) as follows:

$$\frac{\dot{B}}{B} = \beta\left(\frac{\dot{A}}{A}, g\right) \quad \text{or} \quad \beta = \beta(\alpha, g) \quad \text{where} \quad \beta_\alpha < 0, \quad \beta_g > 0, \quad \beta_{\alpha\alpha} < 0. \tag{2.41}$$

The above shows that the tradeoff between labor-augmenting technological progress α and capital-augmenting technological progress β shifts outward (inward) in response to an increase (decrease) in investment per capital stock. Many of innovation's fruits are reaped not only inside firms but also spread over the economy as a whole. In other words, R&D investment has externality effects as its byproduct. The shifts in the innovation possibility frontier are considered to take place as the externality.

2.4.2 *The Long-Run Model and Dynamics*

In view of the equality between investment and saving in (2.19) and (2.20), the growth of capital stock becomes:

$$g = sB\frac{f(k)}{k}. \tag{2.42}$$

Therefore, the differential equation with respect to B becomes:

$$\frac{\dot{B}}{B} = \beta\left(\alpha(k), sB\frac{f(k)}{k}\right), \tag{2.43}$$

and the differential equation with respect to k becomes:

$$\frac{\dot{k}}{k} = sB\frac{f(k)}{k} + \beta\left(\alpha(k), sB\frac{f(k)}{k}\right) - \alpha(k) - \lambda. \tag{2.44}$$

The steady state equilibrium of the system consisting of these two differential equations is given by the solution to the system of the following two equations:

$$\beta\left(\alpha(k^*), sB^*\frac{f(k^*)}{k^*}\right) = 0, \tag{2.45a}$$

$$sB^*\frac{f(k^*)}{k^*} - \alpha(k^*) - \lambda = 0. \tag{2.45b}$$

The stability conditions for steady state equilibrium are as follows:

$$-g\{(1-\theta_K) + \theta_K\beta_g\} - (1-\beta_\alpha)\alpha' < 0, \tag{2.46a}$$

$$\beta_\alpha + \beta_g < 0, \tag{2.46b}$$

where β_α is the partial derivative of $\beta(\cdot)$ with respect to the first argument α, and β_g is the partial derivative with respect to the second argument $g = sBf(k)/k$. Since $\beta_\alpha < 0$ and $\beta_g > 0$, the inequality (2.46a) is surely satisfied. For the inequality (2.46b) to be satisfied, in other words for the steady state equilibrium to be stable, the effect of the investment-capital ratio g on the shift in the innovation possibility frontier β_g cannot dominate its impact on the tradeoff effect along the frontier β_α.

The phase diagram of the system of (2.43) and (2.44) can be depicted in the (k, B) plane as shown in Fig. 2.6. Both the $\dot{B} = 0$ locus and the $\dot{k} = 0$ locus are upward sloping, and the former is steeper than the latter if the inequality (2.46b) holds. If this is the case, the system converges to the steady state, with either monotonic or cyclical behavior.

Suppose that the economy is initially at the steady state and a decline in population growth takes place. As Fig. 2.7 shows, the $\dot{B} = 0$ locus does not change, while the $\dot{k} = 0$ locus shifts downward. In most phases of the transition converging to the new steady state equilibrium, both B and k increase. This implies that the capital share of income decreases with labor-saving technological progress. Comparing the new steady state equilibrium with the initial one, both B and k fall. While the growth rate of capital stock also drops, both the capital-output ratio and the capital share

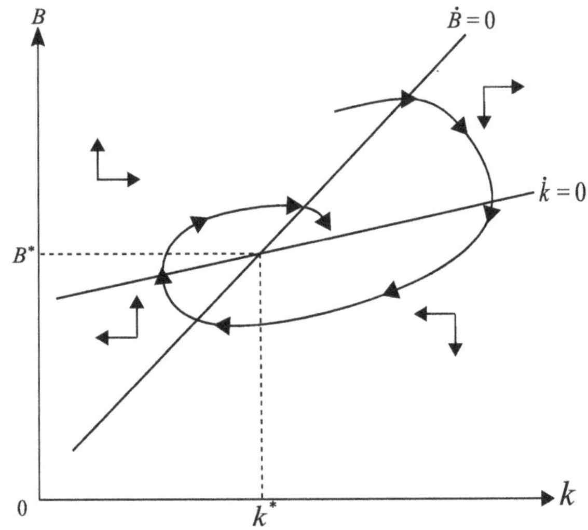

Fig. 2.6 Phase diagram with capital accumulation

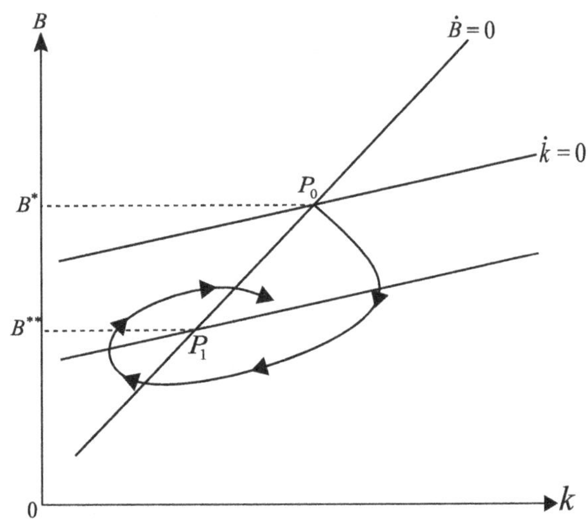

Fig. 2.7 Transition with capital accumulation after a decline in population growth

of income rise. Thus, this model can consistently explain the empirical findings in Piketty (2014).[10]

Next, let us examine the effects of a decline in the saving rate. As Fig. 2.8 shows, although both the $\dot{B} = 0$ and $\dot{k} = 0$ loci shift upward, k at the new steady state must be equal to that at the initial one. Since the decline in the saving rate induces capital-saving technological progress, and hence an increase in B, sB remains unchanged before and after the saving rate decline. As a result, k also remains unchanged.

[10]See Sect. 1.2 in Chap. 1.

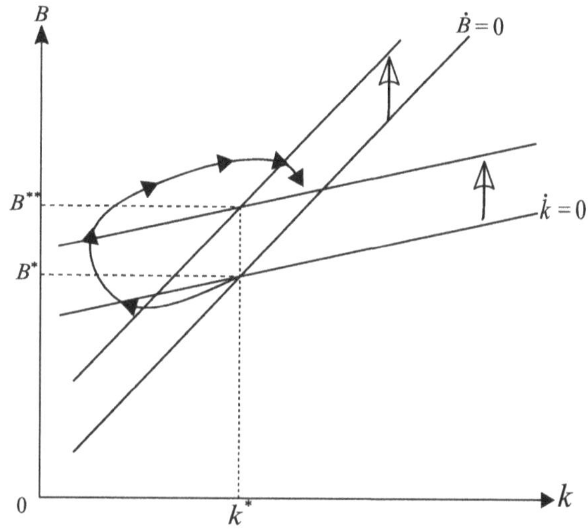

Fig. 2.8 Transition with capital accumulation after a decline in the saving rate

Accordingly, the growth rate of capital stock and the capital share of income do not change, while the capital-output ratio falls.

The above observations lead us to the following proposition.

Proposition 2.5 *Suppose that the innovation possibility frontier is reformulated as* (2.41), *assuming that the frontier shifts outward (inward) in response to an increase (decrease) in investment per capital stock through the externality effect. Then, inequalities* (2.46a) *and* (2.46b) *constitute the stability condition for the dynamic system. Under the stability condition, a decline in population growth decreases the growth of capital stock and income and increases the capital-output ratio and the capital share of income in the long run. Also, a decline in the saving rate decreases the capital-output ratio and does not change the growth of capital stock or income in the long run.*

2.5 Optimal Technological Progress for the Firm and for Society as a Whole[11]

Returning to the model in Sect. 2.3, suppose that the firm maximizes the discounted present value of profits subject to the constraint (2.21). Then, is the type of technological progress chosen by the firm different from the one optimal for society as

[11]Introducing the efficiency wage hypothesis into the induced innovation model, Stiglitz (2014) shows that the market on its own is inefficient, both in the level of unemployment and in the pattern of innovation. However, as the objective function, he uses the maximization of output growth both for the firm's behavior and for social welfare.

a whole? If this is the case, how different is income distribution under the social optimum compared to the one analyzed above? This section deals with these issues.

First, let us compare the two technological progresses in the short run where capital stock K and labor supply N are constant; one is chosen by the firm and the other is the socially optimal one. Since each household supplies one unit of efficient labor, it is plausible to consider that socially optimal technological progress or technological progress that maximizes social welfare is that which maximizes national income subject to the constraint (2.21). Current income being given, maximization of the next period's income by technological progress implies maximization of income growth. Taking constraint (2.21) into account, income growth becomes:

$$\frac{\dot{Y}}{Y} = \{1 - \theta_K(k)\}\frac{\dot{A}}{A} + \theta_K(k)\frac{\dot{B}}{B} = \{1 - \theta_K(k)\}\alpha + \theta_K(k)\beta(\alpha), \tag{2.47}$$

where θ_K is the capital elasticity of output, which is equal to the capital share of income, and a function of the capital-labor ratio $k \equiv BK/AN$, as already shown. Since k is given at any point in time, $\theta_K(k)$ is also given. Denoting α, which maximizes $\dot{Y}/Y$ in (2.47), as α_s, the maximization condition is:

$$\beta'(\alpha_s) = -\frac{1 - \theta_K(k)}{\theta_K(k)}. \tag{2.48}$$

Denoting α, which is determined in the market through the firm's present value of profit maximization as α_m, the maximization condition is

$$\beta'(\alpha_m) = -\frac{1 - \theta_K(k)}{\theta_K(k) - (1 - \sigma)}, \tag{2.49}$$

where $1 - \theta_K(k) < \sigma < 1$ is assumed. From (2.48) and (2.49), $\beta'(\alpha_m) < \beta'(\alpha_s) < 0$. Therefore, $\alpha_m > \alpha_s$ and $\beta(\alpha_m) < \beta(\alpha_s)$. In other words, the technological progress chosen by the firm is more biased toward labor-augmenting (less biased toward capital-augmenting) than the socially optimal one. This implies that, from Harrod's criteria, the technological progress chosen by the firm is too strongly labor-saving compared to the socially optimal one.

So far, we have investigated the properties of choice of technological progress type in the short-run, in which capital stock K and labor supply L are fixed. Next, taking capital accumulation and labor growth into account, let us examine the effects of technological choice on income distribution in the long run. As shown in Sect. 2.2, the type of technological progress chosen by the firm's present value maximization is given by (2.30), and the associated macrodynamic model consists of (2.34) and (2.35). In addition, if $1 - \theta_K(k) < \sigma < 1$ is satisfied, then the dynamic system converges to the steady state determined by (2.38) and (2.39). At the steady state, the technological progress type becomes purely labor-augmenting, and is attained by the horizontal intercept of the innovation possibility frontier, which is $(\bar{\alpha}, 0)$ in Fig. 2.1. Denoting k in the steady state as k^* and considering $\alpha = \bar{\alpha}$, and considering that these variables must satisfy (2.49), the following also holds:

$$\beta'(\bar{\alpha}) = -\frac{1 - \theta_K(k^*)}{\theta_K(k^*) - (1 - \sigma)}. \tag{2.50}$$

On the other hand, the technological progress type that maximizes social welfare is given by (2.48). If this maximization decision repeats continuously at each point in time, then the dynamic system can be shown to converge to the steady state when $\sigma < 1$. Denoting k at the steady state as k^{**}, and considering that $\alpha = \bar{\alpha}$ at the steady state, the maximization condition for social welfare (2.48) must hold as follows:

$$\beta'(\bar{\alpha}) = -\frac{1 - \theta_K(k^{**})}{\theta_K(k^{**})}. \tag{2.51}$$

We come to know from (2.50) and (2.51) that $\theta_K(k^{**}) < \theta_K(k^*)$ and hence $1 - \theta_K(k^{**}) > 1 - \theta_K(k^*)$. In other words, when the firm chooses the type of technological progress so as to maximize the present value of profits, then the capital share of income becomes higher than socially optimal, and hence the labor share is lower than socially optimal in the long run.

The above can be summarized as the following proposition.

Proposition 2.6 *Suppose that the type of technological progress that maximizes the next period's national income, the growth of national income at each point in time, is the socially optimal one. Then, the following properties exist*:

(1) *The type of technological progress chosen by the firm's present value maximization is more labor-augmenting (less capital-augmenting) than the socially optimal one, or is too labor-saving (or too capital-using) from Harrod's criteria.*
(2) *If we compare the steady states attained in the long-run under these two different optimizations, then the long-run capital share of income attained under the firm's present value maximization is higher than that attained under social welfare maximization. The opposite is therefore true for labor's share in income.*

The above proposition shows that the market equilibrium does not necessarily bring about socially optimal outcomes for the income shares. This therefore implies the necessity of such policies in the capital markets as taxation and possible regulation.

2.6 Conclusions

This chapter has constructed a model that modifies existing models at two margins and examined the endogenous determination of technological progress bias and the dynamics of macroeconomic variables. First, although the existing models assume that the type of technological progress is determined by a firm so as to maximize the current cost reduction rate, our model assumes that the firm chooses the type so as to maximize the present value, which is consistent with maximization behavior for determining employment and/or investment. Second, considering the externality effect of investment on technological progress, we have incorporated into the model the hypothesis that the innovation possibility frontier shifts upward (downward) in response to an increase (decrease) in investment.

If we assume present value maximization in determining the type of technological progress, then the labor share of income and the elasticity of substitution between factors play crucial roles. In particular, it has become clear that, if the former exceeds the latter, then labor-saving technological progress is surely chosen, and the choice lowers the labor share. It is also shown that the labor share of income at the steady state depends crucially on the innovation possibility frontier. As long as the frontier is unchanged, population growth has no impact on the income shares at the steady state.

Behind the innovation possibility frontier, there is an implicit assumption that the resource usable for innovation is constant. If a certain portion of investment goes to research and development expenditure, then investment influences the frontier. Introducing investment per capital stock into the model as a shift factor, this chapter has extended the model of induced innovation. The results derived from the model are shown to be consistent with the empirical results in Piketty (2014).

In the last part of this chapter, we investigated the relationship between the optimal type of technological progress for the firm and that for society as a whole. As a result, it is shown that the optimal type for the firm is too labor-augmenting (or too labor-saving in Harrod's sense) compared to the socially optimal one. Also, at the long-run steady state, capital's share of income under the optimal type of technological progress for the firm exceeds that under the optimal type for society as a whole.

Mathematical Appendix

In this mathematical appendix, we prove the following proposition, which is relevant to the firm's maximization in a decision about the direction of technological progress.

Proposition A *Given the time paths of* I_t, K_t *and* $\tilde{k}_t$, *the firm's maximand* (2.27) *with respect to the direction of technological progress is reduced to* $\dot{M} \equiv dM/dt$ *by approximation.*

Proof Since the time path of I_τ, and K_τ for $[t, t{+}h]$ is assumed to be given, maximizing (2.22) is equivalent to maximizing

$$\tilde{V} = \int_t^{t+h} M_\tau K_\tau e^{-r(\tau-t)} d\tau. \tag{2A.1}$$

According to the trapezoidal rule, this maximand is approximated by

$$\tilde{V} = \frac{(M_t K_t + M_{t+h} K_{t+h} e^{-rh})h}{2}. \tag{2A.2}$$

When the firm makes a decision about the direction of technological progress for the time interval $[t, t+h]$ at time t, the initial value $M_t K_t$ and the terminal stock $K_{t+h}e^{-rh}$ are given by assumption. Therefore, maximizing (2A.2) is equivalent to maximizing M_{t+h}. But, when h is sufficiently small, the first order approximation of M_{t+h} is given by

$$M_{t+h} = M_t + h\dot{M}_t, \quad where \quad \dot{M}_t = \frac{dM}{dt}. \tag{2A.3}$$

Since M_t and h are given, maximizing M_{t+h} is reduced to maximizing $\dot{M}_t$. This completes the proof.

Chapter 3
Technological Progress and Unemployment

Abstract By introducing a wage-setting equation derived from efficiency wage or bargaining hypotheses, the standard neoclassical growth model is extended to one where there is persistent unemployment. In this model, if the labor share of income is above (below) the elasticity of substitution between capital and labor, firms tend to introduce labor-saving (capital-saving) technological progress, and the employment rate decreases (increases) as a result. We then develop an induced innovation model including unemployment. We show that (a) if the elasticity of substitution is less than unity but greater than the labor share of income, the steady state with a constant rate of unemployment is stable, but convergence is oscillatory; (b) if the elasticity of substitution is less than the labor share of income, both the employment rate and labor share of income are decreasing under labor-saving technological progress; (c) if the elasticity of substitution is greater than unity, there is a unique steady state equilibrium with a saddle point property. Finally, comparing firms' optimization to social welfare optimization, there will be a bias toward excessive labor-saving technological progress, resulting in unemployment that is too high and a labor share of income that is too low if the elasticity of substitution is less than unity.

Keywords Labor-saving (capital-saving) technological progress
Employment rate · Labor share of income
Elasticity of substitution between labor and capital · Induced innovation

3.1 Introduction

In the previous two chapters, we investigated the effects of technological progress—especially biased technological progress—on growth and income distribution using a standard neoclassical growth model in Chap. 1 and a model of induced invention in Chap. 2. Those models assume that workers are fully employed. In this chapter, we extend the model to one where unemployment exists because of real wage rigidities and study the effects of technological progress on unemployment.

H. Adachi et al., *Technological Progress, Income Distribution, and Unemployment*, Kobe University Social Science Research Series,
https://doi.org/10.1007/978-981-13-3726-0_3

The relationship between technological progress and unemployment has long been a subject of debate. Claims that technological progress causes unemployment tend to emerge when radical technological change occurs. The Luddite movement in the beginning of the nineteenth century is the best known case where significant groups of workers resisted innovation because they regarded modern machines as causes of unemployment and impoverishment. How emerging technology and extensive innovation, such as artificial intelligence (AI), robot technology, the internet of things (IoT), and others will influence employment in the near future is our great concern today. There are two types of technological change and innovation: one is process innovation and the other is product innovation. While process innovation may displace labor and create technological unemployment, product innovation may create new firms and new sectors and thus new jobs. Therefore, the total effects of technological change on unemployment are not so clear.

In this chapter, we analyze the influence of technological progress on employment and income distribution, using a macro growth model that extends the Solow growth model[1] to include the employment rate as an endogenous variable. If the rate of technological progress is constant and labor-augmenting, this model has a unique steady growth equilibrium that satisfies the stability condition, as in the Solow model. In contrast to the Solow model, however, our model includes unemployment even in the steady state equilibrium, which is caused by real wage rigidities arising from efficiency wage concerns or wage bargaining in the labor market. We formulate real wage rigidities in the labor market as the wage-setting equation proposed by Blanchard (1997).[2] In addition, the product market is assumed to be monopolistically competitive. Our growth model is otherwise a neoclassical type, especially in that investment is determined as always equal to saving. With this formulation of the model, we first examine the effects of technological progress on the employment rate under neutral and biased technological progress. We show that depending on whether the labor share of income is above or below the elasticity of substitution between labor and capital, the innovation type chosen by firms becomes labor-saving or capital-saving, and the unemployment rate increases or decreases as a result. We then construct an induced innovation model including unemployment and examine the dynamics of unemployment under induced innovation. In this model, firms choose an innovation type at each point in time to maximize the discounted value of the expected profit. If the elasticity of substitution is less than unity, the system converges with oscillation to the steady state equilibrium that includes a constant rate of unemployment. In the transition to the steady state, labor-saving and capital-saving innovations arise alternately, and the employment rate changes cyclically. Finally, the market solution under firms' optimization is shown to be Pareto inefficient. In particular, compared to the social optimum, we establish there is excessive labor-saving technological change, and that the equilibrium unemployment is too high and the labor share of income is too low.

[1] Solow (1956).

[2] See Blanchard (1997), p. 108.

There are some recent studies that have focused on the relationship between innovation and unemployment. Using an equilibrium search model, Aghion and Howitt (1994) analyze the effects on unemployment of growth that arises from the introduction of new technologies. Pianta (2004) comprehensively surveys literature on this topic and examines the evidence from empirical studies. Stiglitz (2014) uses a model of induced innovation where efficiency wages lead to equilibrium unemployment and shows that if the elasticity of substitution is less than unity, there will be a bias toward excessive labor-augmenting innovation, resulting in too much unemployment. Stiglitz's approach is somewhat similar to ours, but he assumes a fixed coefficient technology when he analyzes the case where unemployment exists. In addition, as is the same with other induced innovation literature, he assumes that firms choose their technologies to maximize "the current rate of cost reduction" for given factor proportions. As Acemoglu et al. (2014) argue, the natural formulation for firms' choice of technologies would be to assume that each firm maximizes the discounted value of its profits.[3]

The rest of the chapter is organized as follows. Section 3.2 extends a neoclassical growth model to one in which unemployment normally exists due to wage and price rigidities. In Sect. 3.3, we derive a dynamic equation with respect to the employment rate and analyze properties of the steady state equilibrium with neutral technological progress. We also examine the effects of wage rigidities and monopoly on the employment rate at the steady state equilibrium. Section 3.4 discusses the decisions of firms on the direction of innovation and the effects on the employment rate. Section 3.5 presents a model of induced innovation including unemployment and examines its dynamics. In Sect. 3.6, we compare firms' optimization to social welfare optimization regarding the direction of innovation and its implications for unemployment and income distribution. Section 3.7 concludes the chapter.

3.2 Model[4]

The production function is assumed to include both labor-augmenting and capital-augmenting technological progress to be represented as follows:

[3]More recently, many studies theoretically or empirically analyze the effects of robots and other computer-assisted technologies on employment, and the labor share of income and wages. For example, see Acemoglu and Restrepo (2017, 2018), Autor and Salmons (2017), Korinek and Stiglitz (2017).

[4]The model in this section is basically the same as Adachi (2009), which is extended in this chapter to analyze the effects of biased technological progress on unemployment.

$$Y = F(AN, BK), \tag{3.1}$$

where Y is output, N is labor employment, K is capital stock, A is the efficiency of labor, and B is the efficiency of capital. Assuming that the production function is subject to constant returns to scale and has other generally assumed properties, we can rewrite it as

$$y = Bf(n) \quad with\ f(0) = 0,\ \ f'(n) > 0,\ \ f''(n) < 0,\ \ f(\infty) = \infty, \tag{3.2}$$

where y is output per unit of capital and n is the labor-capital ratio in efficiency units, that is

$$y \equiv \frac{Y}{K} \quad and \quad n \equiv \frac{AN}{BK}. \tag{3.3}$$

The production function (3.2) expresses output per unit of capital stock as a function of the labor-capital ratio instead of output per unit of labor as a function of the capital-labor ratio, because this form is more convenient for dealing with employment (or unemployment).

We assume, as with the Solow model,[5] that a constant proportion of income is saved and invested. Then, the growth rate of capital is given by the following equation:

$$\frac{\dot{K}}{K} = sBf(n), \tag{3.4}$$

where s represents the saving rate. For simplicity, it is assumed that there is no depletion of capital.

The structure of the model formulated so far is the same as that in the previous two chapters. However, in this chapter, the labor market will be formulated differently than in those two chapters. Instead of assuming that wages and prices are always market-clearing, the model developed in this chapter assumes that wages and prices are more or less sticky due to the behavior of monopolistically competitive firms and the bargaining between firms and workers. The price-setting equation together with the wage-setting equation determine the real wage rate and the employment rate (and so the unemployment rate). The employment rate thus determined is normally less than unity, meaning that unemployment usually exists in the economy.

Let us consider firms' decision on prices and employment. For convenience, we assume that each firm uses one unit of capital. Then, n represents both employment of a firm and employment per unit of capital in efficiency units for the whole economy. As each firm is monopolistically competitive in the goods market, it faces a downward sloping demand curve. The demand for its goods is assumed to be given, in the inverse form, by

[5] See Solow (1956).

$$p = \left(\frac{y}{\bar{y}}\right)^{-\eta}, \quad where \;\; 0 \leq \eta < 1, \tag{3.5}$$

Here, p is the price charged by the firm relative to the price level of the economy, $\bar{y}$ is the average output of all firms, and η is the inverse of the price elasticity of demand.

At each point in time, a firm determines the amount of labor employed to maximize profit π which is expressed as

$$\pi = py - \left(\frac{B}{A}\right)wn, \tag{3.6}$$

where w is the wage rate in terms of the price level of the economy P, which is set equal to unity. The first order condition of profit maximization and the symmetry condition that all firms charge the same price (i.e., $p = 1$) imply that

$$\frac{1}{\mu}f'(n) = \frac{w}{A}, \tag{3.7}$$

where $\mu \equiv 1/(1-\eta)$ is the markup of price over marginal cost. For any given real wage rate, this equation determines each firm's demand for labor. Then, the aggregate demand for labor becomes $N = (B/A)nK$

Let us next consider the supply side of the labor market. In the models presented in the previous two chapters, we assumed that the supply of labor grows at a constant rate independent of the wage rate, and that workers are fully employed through the adjustment of flexible wages and prices. In contrast, in this chapter, we assume that the supply side of the labor market is represented by a wage-setting equation, which makes wages tend to exceed the market-clearing level. The wage-setting equation can be derived from either the bargaining model or the efficiency wage model.[6] Those theoretical models of wage-setting generate a strong core implication that the tighter the labor market, the higher the real wage, given workers' reservation wage. The simplest formulation of wage-setting is given by the following equation, which was proposed by Blanchard (1997)[7]:

$$\frac{w}{A} = \omega\left(\frac{N}{N^s}\right)^{\varepsilon}, \tag{3.8}$$

where N^s is the population of labor, so that N/N^s is the employment rate. The parameter ω represents reservation wages, which reflects the bargaining power of workers. The parameter ε represents the sensitivity of the real wage rate to the tightness of the labor market, and so a larger magnitude of ε implies that the real wage rate is more flexible.

[6] See Layard et al. (2005), pp. 22–30 on this point.

[7] See Blanchard (1997), p. 108.

Denote the ratio of the effective labor population AN^s to effective capital BK by n^s, that is,

$$n^s \equiv \frac{AN^s}{BK}. \tag{3.9}$$

Then, Eq. (3.8) is rewritten, using this and the definition of n in (3.3), as

$$\frac{w}{A} = \omega\left(\frac{n}{n^s}\right)^{\varepsilon}. \tag{3.10}$$

From (3.7) and (3.10), the equilibrium of the labor market is expressed by the following equation:

$$\frac{1}{\mu}f'(n) = \omega\left(\frac{n}{n^s}\right)^{\varepsilon}. \tag{3.11}$$

At a given point in time, n^s is constant if the effective labor population AN^s and effective capital stock BK are given. Thus, this equation determines the equilibrium value of n. It must satisfy the inequality $n \leq n^s$ for this solution to be economically meaningful. We assume that this condition is satisfied in the following. Then, labor employment is determined by $N = (B/A)nK$.

Labor population N^s is assumed here to grow at a constant rate λ, that is,

$$\frac{\dot{N}^s}{N^s} = \lambda. \tag{3.12}$$

The rate of labor-augmenting technological progress is denoted by α, and the rate of capital-augmenting technological progress is denoted by β:

$$\frac{\dot{A}}{A} = \alpha, \quad \frac{\dot{B}}{B} = \beta. \tag{3.13}$$

Taking the time derivative of (3.9) and considering (3.4), (3.12), and (3.13), we have the following dynamic equation:

$$\frac{\dot{n}^s}{n^s} = (\alpha - \beta + \lambda) - sBf(n). \tag{3.14}$$

Given that this equation and (3.11) constitute a complete system for determining the paths of n and n^s, the path of the employment rate n/n^s is also determined.

3.3 Growth and Employment

3.3.1 Dynamics of the Employment Rate

To analyze the relationship between technological progress and unemployment, we rewrite the system consisting of (3.11) and (3.14) in terms of the employment rate. Let us denote the employment rate n/n^s by z:

$$z \equiv \frac{n}{n^s}. \tag{3.15}$$

Then, Eq. (3.11) is rewritten as

$$\frac{1}{\mu}f'(n) = \omega z^{\varepsilon}. \tag{3.16}$$

Taking the logarithmic derivative of this equation with respect to time, we have

$$\frac{\dot{n}}{n} = -\frac{\varepsilon\sigma}{1-\theta_L}\frac{\dot{z}}{z}, \tag{3.17}$$

where θ_L is the elasticity of output with respect to labor and σ is the elasticity of substitution between labor and capital, which are defined as follows[8]:

$$\theta_L \equiv \frac{nf'(n)}{f(n)}, \quad \sigma \equiv -\frac{f'(n)\left[f(n) - nf'(n)\right]}{nf''(n)f(n)}. \tag{3.18}$$

When the production function $f(n)$ has the well-behaved properties as shown in (3.2), these parameters must satisfy $0 < \theta_L < 1$ and $\sigma > 0$.

Differentiation of the definitional Eq. (3.15) with respect to time gives

$$\frac{\dot{z}}{z} = \frac{\dot{n}}{n} - \frac{\dot{n}^s}{n^s}. \tag{3.19}$$

Substituting (3.14) and (3.17) into (3.19) and rearranging it, we have the following equation:

$$\frac{\dot{z}}{z} = \kappa\left[sBf(n) - (\alpha - \beta + \lambda)\right] \quad where \;\; \kappa \equiv \frac{1-\theta_L}{1-\theta_L+\varepsilon\sigma}. \tag{3.20}$$

This equation is reduced to a dynamic equation of z, if the variable n on the right-hand side of this equation is expressed as a function of z. This can be done by solving (3.16) with respect to n as follows:

[8] In Chaps. 1 and 2, we use the notation θ_K as the elasticity of output with respect to capital, that is, $\theta_K \equiv kf'(k)/f(k)$. The relationship between θ_L and θ_K must be $\theta_L \equiv 1 - \theta_K$.

$$n = f'^{-1}(\mu\omega z^{\varepsilon}). \tag{3.21}$$

Since $f'(n)$ is a monotonically decreasing function, n is monotonically decreasing with respect to z. Therefore, $f(n)$ can be transformed into a function of z as follows:

$$f(n) = f(f'^{-1}(\mu\omega z^{\varepsilon})) = \phi(z). \tag{3.22}$$

Since $f(n)$ is a monotonically increasing function and $f'(n)$ is a monotonically decreasing function, $\phi(z)$ becomes a monotonically decreasing function. Substituting (3.22) into (3.20), we obtain a dynamic equation of z as follows:

$$\frac{\dot{z}}{z} = \kappa[sB\phi(z) - (\alpha - \beta + \lambda)] \quad \textit{where} \quad \phi'(z) < 0. \tag{3.23}$$

The dynamics of the employment rate are analyzed using this dynamic equation.

3.3.2 The Steady State Equilibrium and the Employment Rate

We first focus on the case where the dynamic equation (3.23) has the steady-state equilibrium, which occurs when $\beta \equiv \dot{B}/B = 0$. In this case, the steady-state growth rate of national income Y and capital stock K in this model is equal to $\alpha + \lambda$ (the rate of labor-augmenting technological progress plus the rate of population growth):

$$\frac{\dot{Y}}{Y} = \frac{\dot{K}}{K} = \alpha + \lambda. \tag{3.24}$$

The dynamic equation (3.23) is reduced to

$$\frac{\dot{z}}{z} = \kappa[sB\phi(z) - (\alpha + \lambda)], \tag{3.25}$$

and the steady-state equilibrium is attained at z^* such that

$$\phi(z^*) = \frac{\alpha + \lambda}{sB}. \tag{3.26}$$

Figure 3.1 describes the dynamics of z, taking $\dot{z}/z$ on the vertical axis and z on the horizontal axis. Equation (3.25) is represented by the downward sloping curve that intersects the horizontal axis at z^*, the steady-state value of the employment rate. If the employment rate z is initially lower than z^* (e.g., at z_0), it tends to increase, since $\dot{z}/z > 0$ there. The opposite holds if the employment rate z is higher than z^* (e.g., at z_1). Thus, the steady-state equilibrium is stable, so that the dynamic system tends to the steady state from any initial conditions.

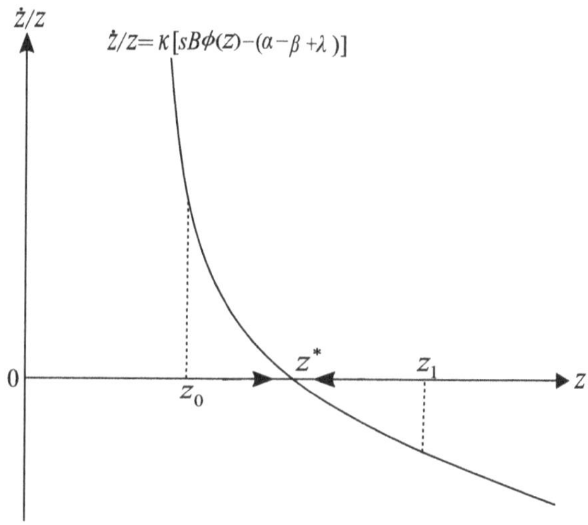

Fig. 3.1 Dynamics of the employment rate and the stability of the steady state

It should be noted here that the capital efficiency coefficient B is explicitly included as a constant parameter in the dynamic Eq. (3.25), as well as in the steady-state equilibrium condition (3.26). By including B explicitly, we can analyze the effects of biased technological change on unemployment and income distribution, as will be shown below. As seen in Chap. 1, a decrease in B means an introduction of labor-saving (capital-using) innovation, and an increase in B introduces capital-saving (labor-using) innovation.

The steady-state growth rate and steady-state employment rate change as the parameters that determine the steady-state equilibrium shift. Therefore, to study the long-run relationship between growth and employment, we should examine shifts in the steady-state equilibrium. As is obvious from Eq. (3.25), if the function ϕ is given, the steady-state employment rate z^* depends on the steady-state growth rate $\alpha + \lambda$, the saving rate s, and the capital efficiency coefficient B. Since $\phi(z)$ is a decreasing function, z^* depends negatively on $\alpha + \lambda$, and positively on s and λ. More strictly, shifts in the steady-state employment rate in response to these parameters are represented by the following equation obtained by taking the difference of both sides of Eq. (3.26)

$$\Delta z^* = \frac{\phi}{\phi'}\left(\frac{\Delta(\alpha+\lambda)}{\alpha+\lambda} - \frac{\Delta B}{B} - \frac{\Delta s}{s}\right). \tag{3.27}$$

Since $\phi/\phi' < 0$, it follows from this equation that

$$\Delta z^* \leq 0 \; or \; \geq 0 \;\; depending \; on \; whether \;\; \frac{\Delta(\alpha+\lambda)}{\alpha+\lambda} - \frac{\Delta B}{B} - \frac{\Delta s}{s} \geq 0 \; or \; \leq 0 \tag{3.28}$$

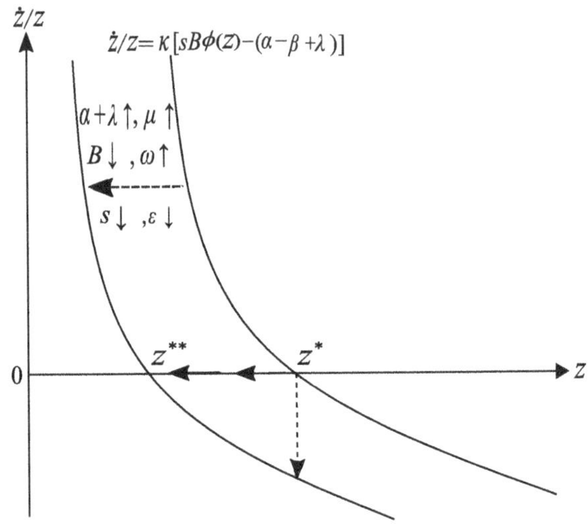

Fig. 3.2 Effects of changes in $\alpha+\lambda$, B, s, μ, ω and ε on the employment rate

This result implies that the steady-state employment rate z^* decreases when any one of the following changes in the parameters occurs: (1) an increase in the steady-state growth rate $\alpha + \lambda$, (2) a decrease in the capital efficiency coefficient B (labor-saving innovation), or (3) a decrease in the saving rate s. The transitional process to the new steady state is depicted in Fig. 3.2. When any one of those changes occurs, the downward sloping curve representing (3.25) shifts downward (or to the left). Then, the value of $\dot{z}/z$ at z^* becomes negative, so that the employment rate z begins to decrease. The decreases in z continues until it reaches the new steady-state employment rate z^{**}.

The result that the steady-state employment rate is negatively related to the steady-state growth rate may seem contrary to what is expected; this result may be interpreted as follows. The steady-state growth rate, $\alpha + \lambda$, represents the growth rate of labor forces in efficiency units. When $\alpha+\lambda$ increases, the steady-state employment-capital ratio in efficiency units n^* increases, since $f(n^*) = (\alpha+\lambda)/sB$. But, when n^* increases, the marginal product of labor in efficiency units $f'(n^*)$ decreases, and so does the real wage rate in efficiency units of labor. Then, the steady-state employment rate z^* decreases in view of the labor market equilibrium (3.16). On the contrary, the steady-state employment rate is positively related to the saving rate s as well as the capital efficiency coefficient B (labor-saving innovation). This is because increases in s or B decrease the steady-state employment-capital ratio in efficiency units n^*.

Proposition 3.1 *The steady-state value of the employment rate z^* is determined by the steady-state growth rate $\alpha + \lambda$, the saving rate s, and the capital efficiency coefficient B. Changes in these parameters cause shifts in the steady-state value of the employment rate in the following way:*

(1) *A decrease in the steady-state growth rate $\alpha + \lambda$ (due to decreases in labor-augmenting technological progress or population growth) increases the employment rate z^*.*
(2) *A decrease in the saving rate s decreases the employment rate z^*.*
(3) *A decrease in the capital efficiency coefficient in B (due to labor-saving innovation) decreases the employment rate z^*.*

3.3.3 Monopoly and the Labor Market

So far, we have ignored the influences of the parameters related to monopoly and the labor market on the properties of the steady state. As is obvious from (3.21), the relationship between n and z depends on such parameters as μ, ω, and ε. Making these parameters explicit, we can rewrite Eq. (3.22) as follows:

$$f(n) = \phi(z; \mu, \omega, \varepsilon), \quad \text{where } \phi_z < 0, \ \phi_\mu < 0, \ \phi_\omega < 0, \ \phi_\varepsilon > 0. \tag{3.29}$$

Then, the steady state equilibrium condition (3.26) is rewritten as

$$\phi(z^*; \mu, \omega, \varepsilon) = \frac{\alpha + \lambda}{sB}. \tag{3.30}$$

So, the effects of changes in μ, ω, and ε on z^* become as follows:

$$\frac{\partial z^*}{\partial \mu} = -\frac{\phi_\mu}{\phi_z} < 0, \quad \frac{\partial z^*}{\partial \omega} = -\frac{\phi_\omega}{\phi_z} < 0, \quad \frac{\partial z^*}{\partial \varepsilon} = -\frac{\phi_\varepsilon}{\phi_z} > 0. \tag{3.31}$$

In other words, if the mark-up rate μ is increased due to a decrease in firm competition in the goods market, the employment rate in the steady state equilibrium will decrease. On the other hand, if the reservation wage ω is increased or the sensitivity of the real wage rate to the tightness of the labor market ε is decreased as a result of an increase in the bargaining power of workers or a rise in the minimum wage rate, the employment rate in the steady state equilibrium will be decreased. Figure 3.2 illustrates these effects with a diagram.

The results obtained above may be summarized as the following proposition.

Proposition 3.2 *The steady state employment rate z^* depends on the parameters related to monopoly and real wage rigidities, μ, ω, ε, and changes in those parameters influence z^* as follows:*

(1) *An increase in the mark-up rate of firms μ decreases z^*.*
(2) *An increase in the reservation wage rate ω decreases z^*.*
(3) *An increase in the sensitivity of real wages to the employment rate ε increases z^*.*

3.4 Biased Technological Progress and Unemployment

3.4.1 Decisions of Firms on the Type of Technological Progress

Suppose that the economy is initially in the steady state, so that technological progress is neutral. In this situation, firms may willingly introduce biased technological progress if it is more profitable to do so. Let us see under what conditions firms are willing to introduce biased technological progress.

Since we assume that firms are monopolistically competitive, in view of (3.2), (3.6), and (3.7), the profit of a firm per unit of capital is given by

$$\pi = B\left\{f(n) - \frac{1}{\mu}nf'(n)\right\}. \tag{3.32}$$

Taking notice of $n \equiv AN/BK$ including B, we have

$$\frac{\Delta\pi}{\Delta B} = f(n)\frac{1-\theta_L}{\sigma}\left(\sigma - \frac{\theta_L}{\mu}\right). \tag{3.33}$$

Here, θ_L is the elasticity of output with respect to labor, σ is the elasticity of substitution between labor and capital, and μ is the mark-up of price over marginal cost. Definitions of θ_L and σ are given by (3.18), and θ_L/μ is equal to the labor share of income. From (3.33), we have

$$\frac{\Delta\pi}{\Delta B} \leq 0 \textit{ or } \frac{\Delta\pi}{\Delta B} \geq 0, \quad \textit{depending on whether } \sigma \leq \frac{\theta_L}{\mu} \textit{ or } \sigma \geq \frac{\theta_L}{\mu}. \tag{3.34}$$

As this result shows, it is more profitable for the firm to introduce labor-saving innovation ($\Delta B < 0$) if the labor share of income exceeds the elasticity of substitution between labor and capital ($\theta_L/\mu > \sigma$), and contrarily, to introduce capital-saving innovation ($\Delta B > 0$) if the labor share of income falls short of the elasticity of substitution between labor and capital ($\theta_L/\mu < \sigma$). Neutral technological progress ($\Delta B = 0$) is profitably sustained if and only if the labor share of income is equal to the elasticity of substitution ($\theta_L/\mu = \sigma$). This result may be summarized by the following proposition.[9]

Proposition 3.3 *Suppose that the economy is initially in the steady state equilibrium so that technological progress is labor-augmenting at a constant rate. In this situation, if the monopolistically competitive firm chooses the type of innovation that maximizes profitability, the type of technology adopted by the firm depends on the relative size of the labor share of income (θ_L/μ) and the elasticity of substitution between labor and capital (σ) is as follows:*

[9]This proposition is the monopolistic competition version of Proposition 1.4 in Chap. 1, and so it differs from the latter by the mark-up factor μ.

(1) *If* $\theta_L/\mu > \sigma$, *labor-saving (capital-using) technological progress is adopted* ($\Delta B < 0$).
(2) *If* $\theta_L/\mu < \sigma$, *capital-saving (labor-using) technological progress is adopted* ($\Delta B > 0$).
(3) *If* $\theta_L/\mu = \sigma$, *neutral technological progress is sustained* ($\Delta B = 0$).

This proposition concerning the introduction of biased technological progress may be formulated as follows:

$$\frac{\dot{B}}{B} = \beta(\sigma - (\theta_L/\mu)), \quad \textit{where} \quad \beta(0) = 0, \quad \beta' > 0. \tag{3.35}$$

It should be noted that labor-augmenting innovation always has positive effects on firms' profitability ($\Delta r/\Delta A > 0$), so higher labor-augmenting technological progress ($\alpha \equiv \dot{A}/A$) is better for firms. As mentioned above, we assume α to be given constant in the discussion in this section.

3.4.2 Effects of Biased Technological Progress on Unemployment

Let us next examine how the introduction of biased technological progress influences the employment rate. Suppose that the economy is initially in the steady state. Then, in view of the dynamic equation (3.25), we must have $\dot{z}/z = 0$ at the employment rate z^* such that

$$sB\phi(z^*) = \alpha + \lambda. \tag{3.36}$$

Then, we have the following results: if $\sigma < \theta_L/\mu$, we have $\dot{B}/B < 0$ from (3.35), so that $\dot{z}/z < 0$ from (3.25); similarly, if $\sigma > \theta_L/\mu$, we have $\dot{B}/B > 0$, so that $\dot{z}/z > 0$; if $\sigma = \theta_L/\mu$, we have $\dot{B}/B = 0$, so that $\dot{z}/z = 0$. These results represent the *immediate* effects of the adoption of biased technological progress on employment and are different from those obtained in Sect. 3.3.2 from the comparison of the steady state. The results may be summarized by the following proposition.

Proposition 3.4 *Suppose that the economy is initially in the steady state. If the monopolistically competitive firm chooses a type of technological progress based on the criterion indicated by* Proposition 3.3, *its immediate effects on the employment rate are as follows*:

(1) *If the labor share of income is higher than the elasticity of substitution between labor and capital* ($\theta_L/\mu > \sigma$), *labor-saving technological progress is adopted* ($\dot{B}/B < 0$), *which results in a decrease in the employment rate* ($\dot{z}/z < 0$).
(2) *If the labor share of income is lower than the elasticity of substitution between labor and capital* ($\theta_L/\mu < \sigma$), *capital-saving technological progress is adopted* ($\dot{B}/B > 0$), *which results in an increase in the employment rate* ($\dot{z}/z > 0$).

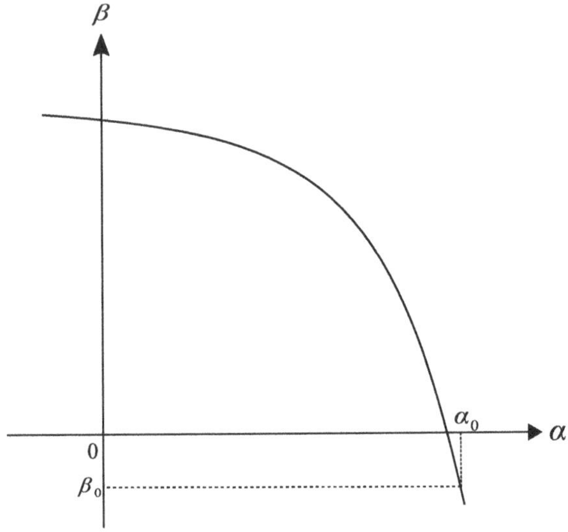

Fig. 3.3 Innovation possibility frontier

(3) *If the labor share of income is equal to the elasticity of substitution between labor and capital* ($\theta_L/\mu = \sigma$), *neutral technological progress* ($\dot{B}/B = 0$) *is sustained, which has no influence on the employment rate* ($\dot{z}/z = 0$).

This proposition suggests that the steady state equilibrium in the model of growth and unemployment presented in Sect. 3.3.2 may not be sustained if firms are allowed to adopt biased technological progress when it is profitable to do so. Introduction of biased innovation influences the employment rate. The steady state equilibrium is sustained if and only if $\theta_L/\mu = \sigma$.

3.5 Induced Innovation and Unemployment

3.5.1 A Model of Innovation and Unemployment

We have so far assumed that the rate of labor-augmenting technological progress α is given constant, and that the firm chooses the rate of capital-augmenting technological progress to maximize the rate of return. If the resources for innovation are given, there may be a trade-off relationship between labor-augmenting technological progress α and capital-augmenting technological progress β. In this section, we make use of the well-established innovation possibility curve, assuming that there is a trade-off between α and β, as depicted in Fig. 3.3 one can only have more capital augmenting technological progress by giving up labor-augmenting technological progress. This relationship is represented as

$$\frac{\dot{B}}{B} = \beta\left(\frac{\dot{A}}{A}\right) \quad or \quad \beta = \beta(\alpha) \quad where \quad \beta' < 0, \quad \beta'' < 0. \tag{3.37}$$

In this section, firms are assumed to be competitive to avoid some unnecessary complications in the following discussion. The competitive firm chooses a type of technological progress from this frontier to maximize the discounted value of the expected return.[10] As we have shown in the previous chapter,[11] if we focus on the determination of types of technological progress, assuming that employment and investment in each period are suitably determined to maximize the discounted value of the expected return, the firm's decision regarding technological progress amounts to maximizing

$$\widetilde{V}_t = \int_t^{t+h} \pi_\tau K_\tau e^{-r(\tau-t)} d\tau, \tag{3.38}$$

subject to (3.37), where

$$\pi_\tau \equiv B_\tau\{f(n_\tau) - n_\tau f'(n_\tau)\} = B_\tau\left\{f\left(\frac{A_\tau N_\tau}{B_\tau K_\tau}\right) - \frac{A_\tau N_\tau}{B_\tau K_\tau} f'\left(\frac{A_\tau N_\tau}{B_\tau K_\tau}\right)\right\}. \tag{3.39}$$

In this case, it is shown that maximizing (3.38) with respect to α subject to (3.37) is equivalent to maximizing $\dot{\pi} \equiv d\pi_t/dt$ with respect to α under the same constraint.[12] With fixed N_t and K_t, we have

$$\dot{\pi} = \pi\left(1 - \frac{\theta_L(n)}{\sigma}\right)\frac{\dot{B}}{B} + \frac{\theta_L(n)}{\sigma}\frac{\dot{A}}{A} = \frac{\pi}{\sigma}[\{\sigma - \theta_L(n)\}\beta(\alpha) + \theta_L(n)\alpha]. \tag{3.40}$$

The maximizing condition of this expression with respect to α is

$$\frac{\partial\dot{\pi}}{\partial\alpha} = \frac{\pi}{\sigma}\left[\{\sigma - \theta_L(n)\}\beta'(\alpha) + \theta_L(n)\right] = 0. \tag{3.41}$$

Hence, with fixed n, the type of technological progress that maximizes the discounted value of the expected return V is given by α that satisfies the following condition:

---

[10] In the prototypical model of induced innovation (e.g., Kennedy (1964), Drandakis and Phelps (1965)), firms are assumed to hire the profit-maximizing amount of factors, while they choose their technologies to maximize the current rate of cost reduction for given factor proportions. In our model, firms are assumed to maximize profit in both decisions.

[11] See Sects. 2.2 and 2.3 of Chap. 2 for this point, noting that $n_t \equiv 1/k_t$.

[12] The proof of this statement is given in the mathematical appendix in Chap. 2.

$$\beta'(\alpha) = -\frac{\theta_L(n)}{\sigma - \theta_L(n)}. \tag{3.42}$$

Since $\beta'(\alpha) < 0$ and $0 < \theta_L(n) < 1$, this condition gives a meaningful solution if and only if $\theta_L(n) < \sigma$. We first discuss the case where this condition is satisfied and deal with the case of $\theta_L(n) \geq \sigma$ later.

When the condition $\theta_L(n) < \sigma < 1$ is satisfied, α can be expressed as an increasing function of $\theta_L(n)$ as follows:

$$\alpha = \psi(\theta_L(n)), \quad \textit{with} \;\; \psi' > 0. \tag{3.43}$$

As for $\theta_L(n)$, by taking its derivative, it is shown that

$$\theta_L'(n) = \theta_L(n)\{1 - \theta_L(n)\}\frac{\sigma - 1}{\sigma} < 0 \textit{ or } > 0 \;\; \textit{according to} \;\; \sigma < 1 \textit{ or } > 1. \tag{3.44}$$

In addition, in view of (3.22), n is expressed as a decreasing function of z as follows:

$$n = \xi(z), \quad \textit{with} \;\; \xi' < 0. \tag{3.45}$$

From (3.43), (3.44), and (3.45), α becomes a function of z with the following property:

$$\alpha = \alpha(z), \quad \textit{with} \;\; \alpha' = \psi'\theta_L'\xi > 0 \textit{ or } < 0 \textit{ according to } \sigma < 1 \textit{ or } > 1 \tag{3.46}$$

Substituting this function into the innovation possibility frontier (3.37), we can express it as a function of z with the following property:

$$\frac{\dot{B}}{B} = \beta(\alpha(z)) \;\; \textit{where} \;\; \beta'\alpha' < 0 \textit{ or } > 0 \;\; \textit{depending on whether } \sigma < 1 \textit{ or } > 1. \tag{3.47}$$

This equation shows how the bias in technological progress depends on the employment rate. Substituting this equation into the dynamic equation for the employment rate (3.23), we have

$$\frac{\dot{z}}{z} = \kappa[sB\phi(z) - \{\alpha(z) - \beta(\alpha(z)) + \lambda\}]. \tag{3.48}$$

The two dynamic Eqs. (3.47) and (3.48) constitute a complete system that explains interactions between the employment rate z and the bias in technological progress B.

This complete system is applicable to the case $\theta_L < \sigma$ where an interior maximum solution exists for (3.41). Let us next examine the case where $\theta_L \geq \sigma$ holds. In this case, in view of (3.42), $\dot{\pi}$ becomes larger as α increases. This implies that the firm can obtain maximum profit by choosing the maximum possible value of α. Let the maximum value of α on the innovation possibility curve be α_0. Then, the corner point on the innovation possibility curve $(\alpha_0, \beta(\alpha_0))$ represents the optimum type of technological progress chosen by the firm.[13] At the corner point, we have $\beta(\alpha_0) < 0$, which means that technological progress is labor-saving. The complete dynamic system in this case becomes

$$\frac{\dot{B}}{B} = \beta(\alpha_0) < 0, \tag{3.49}$$

$$\frac{\dot{z}}{z} = \kappa[sB\phi(z) - \{\alpha_0 - \beta(\alpha_0) + \lambda\}]. \tag{3.50}$$

In the following section, we examine the properties of those two systems and see how they are related.

3.5.2 Dynamics and Unemployment: The Case of $\sigma < 1$

Let us first consider the case where the rate of substitution between labor and capital is less than unity ($\sigma < 1$). In this case, in view of (3.44) and (3.45), θ_L becomes an increasing function of z. If we denote this functional relationship as $\theta_L = \theta_L(z)$, then $\theta_L'(z) > 0$ in the domain of z, $0 \le z \le 1$. Then, there exists a unique value of z, denoted by $\bar{z}$, such that $\theta_L(\bar{z}) = \sigma$, and that $\theta_L(z) < \sigma < 1$ for $z < \bar{z}$ and $\theta_L(z) > \sigma$ for $z > \bar{z}$. As discussed in the last section, the dynamic system of (3.47) and (3.48) applies for the case $\theta_L(z) < \sigma$, and that of (3.49) and (3.50) applies for the case $\theta_L(z) \ge \sigma$. Therefore, (3.47) and (3.48) applies for $z < \bar{z}$, and (3.49) and (3.50) applies for $z \ge \bar{z}$.

First, we examine the case where $\theta_L(z) < \sigma < 1$ holds, and so z is in the range $z < \bar{z}$. In this case, the dynamic system consists of (3.47) and (3.48), which has the steady state equilibrium (z^*, B^*) given by the following two equations:

$$\beta(\alpha(z^*)) = 0, \tag{3.51}$$

$$B^* = \frac{\alpha(z^*) - \beta(\alpha(z^*)) + \lambda}{s\phi(z^*)}. \tag{3.52}$$

Equation (3.51) can be solved uniquely for z^* if $\sigma < 1$. Given z^*, Eq. (3.52) is solved uniquely for B^*. Figure 3.4 provides a diagrammatic solution. The locus for $\dot{B}/B = 0$ is a vertical line at $z = z^*$. On the other hand, differentiating (3.52) logarithmically and considering (3.23), (3.46), and (3.47), it is shown that

$$\frac{1}{B}\frac{dB}{dz} = \frac{\alpha'(z) - \beta'(\alpha)\alpha'(z)}{\alpha(z) - \beta(\alpha(z)) + \lambda} - \frac{\phi'(z)}{\phi'(z)} > 0 \quad if \quad \sigma < 1; \tag{3.53}$$

[13]See Fig. 3.3.

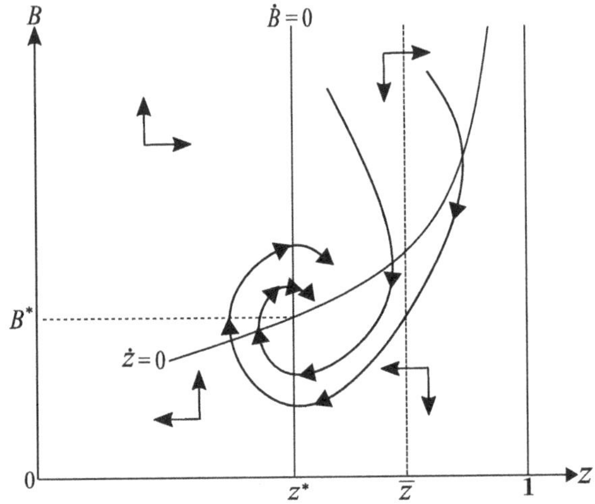

Fig. 3.4 Dynamics of the induced innovation model with unemployment: the case $\sigma < 1$

in other words, if the elasticity of substitution is less than unity, (3.52) is an upward sloping curve. As illustrated in Fig. 3.4, the phase diagram shows an oscillatory convergence to the equilibrium.

Next, we consider the case $\theta_L(z) \geq \sigma$, and so $z \geq \bar{z}$. In this case, the dynamic system is represented by (3.49) and (3.50). In Fig. 3.4, the upward sloping curve in the range $z \geq \bar{z}$ depicts the locus of $\dot{z}/z = 0$, that is,

$$B = \frac{\alpha_0 - \beta(\alpha_0) + \lambda}{s\phi(z)}. \tag{3.54}$$

Above this locus, z is increasing, and below it, z is decreasing. On the other hand, in view of (3.49), B is always decreasing in this phase, since $\dot{B}/B < 0$ for $z \geq \bar{z}$. As Fig. 3.4 shows, if the economy is initially in this phase, B is decreasing and z is also decreasing sooner or later. This means that the employment rate is decreasing (unemployment is increasing) and the labor share of income θ_L is also decreasing under labor-saving innovation. Sooner or later, the economy will move to the range $z < \bar{z}$, and then converge to the steady state equilibrium with oscillation.

3.5.3 Dynamics and Unemployment: The Case of $\sigma > 1$

The dynamic system in this case consists of (3.47) and (3.48), and its steady state equilibrium is given by (3.51) and (3.52). However, contrary to the case of $\sigma < 1$, $\theta_L'(z)$ is a decreasing function and $\alpha'(z)$ is a decreasing function. As shown in Fig. 3.5, the steady state in this case is an unstable saddle point, with the economy normally diverging either to a situation where $z = 0$ *or* 1 and $\theta_L = 0$ *or* 1. If the economy gets into a situation where the employment rate is too high, and the labor share of income

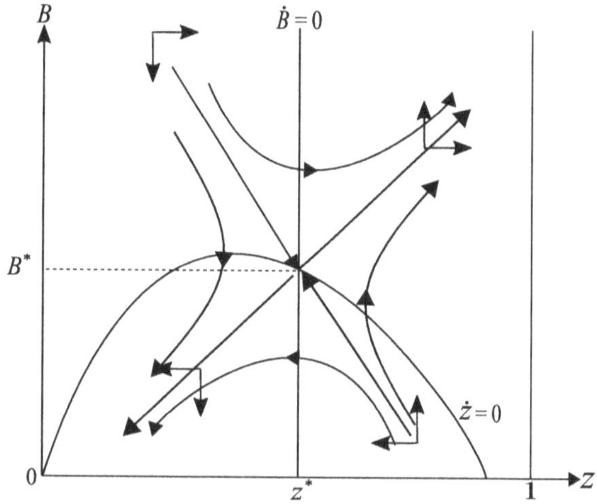

Fig. 3.5 Dynamics of the induced innovation model with unemployment: the case $\sigma > 1$

is also too high (above the equilibrium trajectories going into (z^*, B^*)), technology becomes capital-saving, leading the employment rate to increase still further. On the other hand, if the economy is initially at any value of (z, B) below the equilibrium trajectory, z and B both approach zero.

The above results may be summarized by the following propositions.

Proposition 3.5 *Suppose that the bias in technological progress is endogenously determined under firms' profit maximizing behavior. Then, the economy is stable if the elasticity of substitution between labor and capital is less than unity, but convergence to the steady state may not be monotonic. On the other hand, the economy is dynamically unstable if the elasticity of substitution is greater than unity.*

Proposition 3.6 *If the elasticity of substitution is less than unity, there exists a unique value of the employment rate $\bar{z}$ such that $\theta_L(\bar{z}) = \sigma$, and that $\theta_L(z) < \sigma < 1$ for $z < \bar{z}$ and $\theta_L(z) \geq \sigma$ for $z \geq \bar{z}$. Dynamics of the economy in each phase are as follows:*

(1) *If the economy is initially in the phase $z < \bar{z}$, and so $\theta_L(z) < \sigma < 1$, there exists a steady state equilibrium satisfying* (3.51) *and* (3.52)*, to which the economy converges oscillatorily.*
(2) *If the economy is initially in the phase $z \geq \bar{z}$, and so $\theta_L(z) \geq \sigma$, technological progress is always labor-saving; the employment rate and labor share of income are decreasing in almost all parts of this phase. Sooner or later, the economy moves into the phase where $z < \bar{z}$ and $\theta_L(z) < \sigma < 1$, and in the long-run converges to the steady state equilibrium.*

3.6 Profit Maximization Versus Social Welfare Maximization

So far, we have assumed that the type of technological progress is determined by firms to maximize profit. In this section, we examine how this technological progress differs from that which maximizes social welfare and see what differences there will be in income distribution and unemployment between profit maximization and social welfare maximization.

How is social welfare maximizing technological progress defined? Assuming that the costless redistribution of income is possible, social welfare is maximized by maximizing national output with respect to the technology type subject to the innovation possibility curve. Given the national output at present, maximizing that of the next period is equivalent to maximizing its growth rate. With fixed K and N, the growth rate of national output due to technological progress under the constraint of the innovation possibility curve (3.37) is given by[14]

$$\frac{\dot{Y}}{Y} = \theta_L(z)\frac{\dot{A}}{A} + \{1 - \theta_L(z)\}\frac{\dot{B}}{B} = \{1 - \theta_L(z)\}\beta(\alpha) + \theta_L(z)\alpha, \tag{3.55}$$

where θ_L is the labor elasticity of output expressed as a function of the employment rate z. Since z is given at a point in time, $\theta_L(z)$ is also given. Maximizing (3.55) with respect to α, we obtain the following social welfare maximizing condition:

$$\beta'(\alpha_s) = -\frac{\theta_L(z)}{1 - \theta_L(z)}, \tag{3.56}$$

where α_s is the welfare optimizing value of α.

On the other hand, the condition for profit maximization of firms is expressed by (3.42), that is,

$$\beta'(\alpha) = -\frac{\theta_L(z)}{\sigma - \theta_L(z)}. \tag{3.57}$$

Here we assume the market to be perfectly competitive instead of monopolistically competitive to simplify the analysis. We also assume that Eq. (3.57) has an interior solution. In this case, the condition $\theta_L(z) < \sigma < 1$ must be satisfied. Then, from (3.56) and (3.57), we have $\beta'(\alpha) < \beta'(\alpha_s) < 0$, which implies $\alpha > \alpha_s$ and $\beta(\alpha) < \beta(\alpha_s)$. In other words, profit maximizing innovation is excessively labor-augmenting compared to socially optimal innovation. In terms of Harrod's criterion, it is excessively labor saving.

---

[14]Maximizing the rate of output growth taking K and N as given is equivalent to maximizing the current rate of cost reduction for given K and N. The induced innovation literature, such as Kennedy (1964) and Drandakis and Phelps (1965) used this objective function for firms' decisions on technologies. However, this objective function should rather be interpreted as social welfare maximization. See footnote 10.

The above result shows the properties of the innovation type chosen in the short-run with fixed K and N. Next, with this innovation type, let us examine what happens to income distribution and unemployment in the long-run when capital accumulation and growth of labor are considered. With profit maximization of firms, the innovation type is determined by (3.42), and the dynamic system in this case consists of (3.47) and (3.48). This dynamic system converges to the steady state represented by (3.51) and (3.52), if the condition $\theta_L(z) < \sigma < 1$ is satisfied. At the steady state, technological progress is purely labor-augmenting, which is attained at the intersection of the innovation possibility curve with the horizontal axis, that is, $(\bar{\alpha}, 0)$ in Fig. 3.1. Thus, Eq. (3.42) in the steady state is indicated by

$$\beta'(\bar{\alpha}) = -\frac{\theta_L(z^*)}{\sigma - \theta_L(z^*)}, \tag{3.58}$$

where z^* denotes the steady state value of z.

On the other hand, if the social welfare maximizing condition (3.56) is sustained with dynamics (3.47) and (3.48), it is shown that the system converges to the steady state if $\sigma < 1$. Taking into account $\alpha_s = \bar{\alpha}$ in the steady state, and denoting the socially optimal steady state value of z by z^{**}, the welfare maximizing condition (3.56) that must be satisfied in the steady state becomes as follows:

$$\beta'(\bar{\alpha}) = -\frac{\theta_L(z^{**})}{1 - \theta_L(z^{**})}. \tag{3.59}$$

Comparing (3.58) with (3.59), we obtain $\theta_L(z^*) < \theta_L(z^{**})$, so that $z^* < z^{**}$. In other words, the innovation type chosen by firms to maximize their profits brings about a lower share of income for labor and a lower employment rate in the long-run than the socially optimal levels.

The above result may be summarized by the following proposition.

Proposition 3.7 *Given the innovation possibility curve, the socially optimal innovation type is defined as that which maximizes national output in the next period, which is equivalent to maximizing the growth rate of national output from the present period to the next. If the elasticity of substitution between labor and capital σ is less than unity, the innovation type chosen by firms to maximize their profits has the following properties compared with socially optimal innovation:*

(1) *The innovation type is excessively labor-augmenting compared to the socially optimal one, which implies excessively labor-saving in terms of Harrod's criterion.*
(2) *The labor share of income and the employment rate in the steady state equilibrium attained in the long-run are both lower than the socially optimal level.*

Thus, if social welfare is concerned with the distribution of income (inequality) or unemployment, the market will lead to excessively labor-augmenting innovation if the elasticity of substitution is less than unity.

3.7 Conclusions

In the standard neoclassical growth model, it is assumed that there is always full employment with perfectly competitive markets. Therefore, the relationship between technological progress and unemployment, a subject of great importance today, cannot be analyzed with this model. In this chapter, we extended the standard neoclassical growth model to one where there is persistent unemployment due to real wage rigidities. We formulated real wage rigidities using a wage-setting equation that can be derived from efficiency wage or bargaining hypotheses. Our model includes unemployment even in the steady state equilibrium under neutral technological progress.

Using this model, we showed that if the labor share of income is above (below) the elasticity of substitution between labor and capital in the steady state, firms introduce labor-saving (capital-saving) technological progress, and the employment rate decreases (increases) as a result. Then, we developed an induced innovation model including unemployment, and analyzed optimal decisions and dynamics on the factor bias of innovation and the employment rate. We showed that (a) if the elasticity of substitution is greater than the labor share of income and less than unity, there is a unique steady state equilibrium with a constant employment rate and it is stable, but convergence is oscillatory; (b) if the elasticity of substitution is less than the labor share of income, the employment rate and the labor share of income are always decreasing under labor-saving technological progress, so that labor's share of income falls below the elasticity of substitution sooner or later and convergence to the steady state takes place; (c) if the elasticity of substitution is greater than unity, there is a unique steady state equilibrium which is a saddle point. Finally, comparing firms' optimization to social welfare optimization on the factor bias of innovation, we showed that if the elasticity of substitution is less than unity, there will be a bias toward excessive labor-saving technological progress, resulting in unemployment that is too high and a labor share of income that is too low.

Chapter 4
Empirical Analysis of Biased Technological Progress

Abstract This chapter investigates the empirical adequacy of several propositions and assumptions provided in earlier chapters. The novelty of our empirical analysis is the proposal of a new econometric procedure to estimate the efficiency coefficients of labor and capital (A and B) *separately*, and this procedure is applied to data for Japan. First, we find that the elasticity of substitution between capital and labor is less than 1. Second, the growth rate of B is negative on average over the sample period 1994–2012, which suggests that labor-saving technological progress is introduced from the theoretical perspective developed in earlier chapters. Third, the growth rate of B is negative, as the labor share of income is higher than the elasticity of substitution. Fourth, the labor share of income is adjusted toward the value of the elasticity of substitution over the sample period. Fifth, the unemployment rate increases (decreases) as the labor share of income is larger (smaller) than the elasticity of substitution.

Keywords Efficiency coefficients · Elasticity of substitution
Labor share of income · Biased technological progress · Unemployment

4.1 New Procedure for Estimation of Efficiency Coefficients and Elasticity of Substitution

4.1.1 Model

The theoretical propositions in earlier chapters are mainly based on two factors: the elasticity of substitution between capital and labor (σ) and the efficiency coefficients of capital and labor. Because they are unobservable, we need to estimate these factors to examine the validity of the propositions. Our estimation procedure involves the following two steps:

H. Adachi et al., *Technological Progress, Income Distribution, and Unemployment*,
Kobe University Social Science Research Series,
https://doi.org/10.1007/978-981-13-3726-0_4

(i) The structural parameters of the production function, including σ, are estimated based on a regression model that is derived by combining the first-order conditions for labor and capital.
(ii) We substitute the estimated structural parameters of the production function and the actual values of labor, capital, and their prices into the first-order conditions for labor and capital, respectively. These two equations then include only A and B as unknown values. Therefore, time-series observations of A and B can be separately back-calculated from the first-order conditions.

The idea for the second step is fundamentally the same as the calculation of the Solow residual. The main results are summarized in Table 4.1.

Closely related empirical studies are Oberfield and Raval (2014), Sato (1970), Sato and Morita (2009). Oberfield and Raval (2014) use U.S. cross-sectional data for more than 180,000 enterprises, and their estimate for the elasticity of substitution between labor and capital is constructed from various parameters, such as the price elasticity of demand and the elasticity of substitution between materials and non-materials. Therefore, their estimation procedure for technological progress is much more complicated compared to our approach, which requires only the parameters of the production function.

Using production functions, Sato (1970) demonstrates the dynamics of A and B over the period 1910–1960, and this result is updated to 2004 by Sato and Morita (2009). Their approach strongly depends on the structural parameters of production functions, especially the elasticity of substitution between labor and capital. Our procedure is similar in this respect, but a significant difference is that our procedure enables us to estimate the elasticity of substitution as well as A and B.[1] Since our procedure is based on the structure of the production function, the joint estimation of A, B, and σ may provide more accurate results.

A specific explanation for our estimation procedure for A, B, and σ is as follows. Firms produce output using an aggregate technology that takes a standard constant elasticity of substitution (CES) form as

$$Y_t = \left[\alpha(B_t K_t)^{\frac{\sigma-1}{\sigma}} + (1-\alpha)(A_t N_t)^{\frac{\sigma-1}{\sigma}}\right]^{\frac{\sigma}{\sigma-1}}, \tag{4.1}$$

where Y_t denotes aggregate output; K_t, aggregate capital; N_t, aggregate labor; and α, a positive parameter. Assuming that firms operate in perfect competition, the first-order conditions for profit maximization are

[1] Using the assumption of Hicks-neutral technical progress, Sato and Morita (2009) calculate the elasticity of substitution as the average of the growth rate difference between capital and labor divided by the corresponding growth rate difference of factor prices.

Table 4.1 Summary of this chapter

Propositions or key assumptions in earlier chapters	Empirical findings Contents of this chapter
Chapter 1, Assumption: The elasticity of substitution between capital and labor is less than 1	*Section* 4.1. *Estimation of elasticity of substitution* We find that the elasticity of substitution between capital and labor is 0.657
Proposition 1.1: When the elasticity of substitution between capital and labor is less than 1, labor-saving technological progress is introduced if the growth rate of the efficiency coefficient of capital (B) is negative	*Section* 4.2. *Estimation of efficiency coefficients* Time-series observations of B are calculated using our new procedure. The growth rate of B is found to be negative on average over the sample period 1994–2012 The efficiency coefficient of labor (A) is also calculated using the same procedure, and its growth rate is positive for the sample period
Proposition 1.4: If the labor share of income is larger (smaller) than the elasticity of substitution between capital and labor, the growth rate of B is negative (positive) because of the introduction of labor-saving (capital-saving) technology	*Section* 4.3. *Introduction of Biased Technology* The difference between the labor share of income and the estimated value of the elasticity of substitution is used as an explanatory variable, and an explained variable is B, calculated in Sect. 4.2. We find that the regression coefficient is significantly negative
Proposition 1.5: The labor share of income decreases as this variable is larger than the elasticity of substitution between capital and labor, and vice versa. Consequently, the labor share of income is adjusted toward the value of the elasticity of substitution in the long run	*Section* 4.4 *Interpretation for the labor share of income* The labor share of income in Japan is adjusted toward the elasticity of substitution between labor and capital over the full-sample period 1973–2012. The labor share of income was much higher than the elasticity of substitution in the late 1970s but declined very quickly from the 1980s. After the 1990s, this variable fluctuated stably around the value of the elasticity of substitution
Chapter 2, Assumption: A trade-off exists between the rates of labor-augmenting and capital-augmenting technological progresses (i.e., the innovation possibility frontier)	*Section* 4.5. *Estimation of technology trade-off* We examine the relationship between the growth rates of the efficiency coefficients of capital and labor, which are calculated using our new procedure in Sect. 4.2. This relationship is found to be negative, suggesting the existence of the innovation possibility frontier
Proposition 3.4: If the labor share of income is higher than the elasticity of substitution between labor and capital, labor-saving innovation is adopted and the unemployment rate increases However, if the labor share of income is smaller than the elasticity of substitution, capital-saving innovation is adopted and the unemployment rate decreases	*Section* 4.6. *Effect of innovation on unemployment* The difference between the labor share of income and the estimated value of the elasticity of substitution is used as an explanatory variable, and the explained variable is the unemployment rate. We find that the regression coefficient is significantly positive. Therefore, the proposition holds

$$\frac{Y_t}{K_t} = \alpha^{-\sigma} r_t^{\sigma} B_t^{1-\sigma}, \tag{4.2}$$

$$\frac{Y_t}{N_t} = (1-\alpha)^{-\sigma} w_t^{\sigma} A_t^{1-\sigma}, \tag{4.3}$$

where w_t is the real wage rate, and r_t is the real interest rate. Combining (4.2) and (4.3) gives

$$\frac{r_t K_t}{w_t N_t} = \left(\frac{\alpha}{1-\alpha}\right)^{\sigma} \left(\frac{r_t}{w_t}\right)^{1-\sigma} \left(\frac{A_t}{B_t}\right)^{1-\sigma}. \tag{4.4}$$

Our estimation procedure of σ, A_t, and B_t is based on Eqs. (4.2)–(4.4) as mentioned below.

Step 1. *Estimation of σ*

Using Eq. (4.4), we obtain the following equation in logarithmic form:

$$\ln\left(\frac{r_t K_t}{w_t N_t}\right) = \sigma \ln\left(\frac{\alpha}{1-\alpha}\right) + (1-\sigma)\ln\left(\frac{r_t}{w_t}\right) + (1-\sigma)\ln\left(\frac{A_t}{B_t}\right). \tag{4.5}$$

This equation can be rewritten as a regression model

$$\ln\left(\frac{r_t K_t}{w_t N_t}\right) = \beta_0 + \beta_1 \ln\left(\frac{r_t}{w_t}\right) + e_t, \tag{4.6}$$

where $\beta_0 \equiv \sigma \ln\left(\frac{\alpha}{1-\alpha}\right)$, $\beta_1 \equiv 1-\sigma$, and $e_t \equiv (1-\sigma)\ln\left(\frac{A_t}{B_t}\right)$. Note that the error term e_t includes information about unobservable variables A_t and B_t. Since from a theoretical perspective these variables are strongly associated with factor prices r_t and w_t, endogeneity problems are likely to occur in Eq. (4.6). Therefore, it is preferable to use instrumental variable techniques when we estimate regression coefficients β_0 and β_1.

The structural parameters of the production function are calculated as

$$\sigma = 1 - \beta_1, \tag{4.7}$$

$$\alpha = \frac{\exp\left(\frac{\beta_0}{1-\beta_1}\right)}{1+\exp\left(\frac{\beta_0}{1-\beta_1}\right)}. \tag{4.8}$$

Step 2. *Estimation of A_t and B_t*

Using Eqs. (4.2) and (4.3), we obtain

$$\ln(B_t) = \frac{\sigma}{1-\sigma}\ln(\alpha) + \frac{1}{1-\sigma}\ln\left(\frac{Y_t}{K_t}\right) - \frac{\sigma}{1-\sigma}\ln(r_t), \tag{4.9}$$

$$\ln(A_t) = \frac{\sigma}{1-\sigma}\ln(1-\alpha) + \frac{1}{1-\sigma}\ln\left(\frac{Y_t}{N_t}\right) - \frac{\sigma}{1-\sigma}\ln(w_t). \tag{4.10}$$

Let us assume that observations of K_t, r_t, N_t, w_t, and Y_t are available. Then, substituting these observations and the estimated structural parameters σ and α into the first-order conditions (4.9) and (4.10), we can back-calculate A_t and B_t separately.

Note that the availability of data for capital K_t and its price r_t is crucial in conducting our estimation procedure because observations of these variables are not officially reported in many countries. In the case of Japan, the Research Institute of Economy, Trade and Industry (RIETI) and the Cabinet Office publish the data on these variables, and therefore, our procedure can easily be applied to Japanese data.

4.1.2 Data

Data on capital costs $r_t K_t$ are available from the database of the RIETI, but the rate of return on capital r_t is not available, making it difficult to calculate A_t and B_t. Hence, in the second step, we use data from the Cabinet Office, which publishes data on the rental price of capital. The estimation results for A_t and B_t are reported in Sect. 4.2.

In this study, we use annual data because of data availability. Data from the RIETI are used to estimate Eq. (4.6). Data from the RIETI (JIP database) are available from 1970, but the data from the Cabinet Office are available from 1994. To increase the sample size, we prefer to use the former data when estimating Eq. (4.5). The sample period is from 1970 to 2012. Details on the data are reported in Table 4.2.

Data for the real estate sector are unavailable. Therefore, data for the total economy excluding the real estate sector are used.

4.1.3 Estimation Results of σ

To correct for endogeneity and serial correlation in Eq. (4.6), we use the generalized method of moments (GMM) developed by Hansen (1982). Before estimating

Table 4.2 Data

Variable	Data
rK	Capital costs
wN	Labor costs
r	Capital costs divided by net capital stock
w	Labor costs divided by number of workers

Eq. (4.6), it is necessary to examine the unit root properties of the variables because the GMM technique is applicable to stationary time series data. In this study, we use the unit root test developed by Phillips and Perron (1988).

The results are reported in Table 4.3. The null hypothesis of a unit root is rejected for all variables, suggesting that they are stationary. Therefore, we can use the GMM technique to estimate Eq. (4.6).

The estimation results are reported in Table 4.4. We find that all parameters are significant at the 5 percent level, and this result is consistent with the theoretical model presented in Sect. 4.1.1. Furthermore, the validity of overidentifying restrictions is not rejected, and the null hypothesis of weak instruments is rejected. These diagnostic tests suggest that Eq. (4.6) is successfully estimated.

Substituting the estimation results of β_0 and β_1 into Eqs. (4.7) and (4.8), we find that the elasticity of substitution between capital and labor is 0.657. Therefore, we

Table 4.3 Unit root test

Variable	Statistic
$\ln(r_t K_t) - \ln(w_t N_t)$	–4.175**
$\ln(r_t) - \ln(w_t)$	–4.535***

The unit root test includes a constant term and a linear trend. The spectral estimation method used is the Bartlett kernel, and the bandwidth parameter is selected by the Newey and West (1994) procedure

*** and **indicate significance at the 1% and 5% levels, respectively

Table 4.4 GMM estimation results for the structural parameters of the production function

(A) Estimation results		
Parameter	Estimate	Standard error
β_0	–0.439**	0.194
β_1	0.343**	0.131
α	0.339	NA
σ	0.657	NA
(B) Diagnostic tests		
J-statistic		2.963 (0.397)
Cragg-Donald F-statistic		44.120

The set of instruments includes $\ln(r_t K_t)-\ln(w_t N_t)$ and $\ln(r_t)-\ln(w_t)$ with 1 and 2 lags and a constant term. Heteroskedasticity and autocorrelation consistent (HAC) standard errors are reported. The spectral estimation method used is the Bartlett kernel, and the bandwidth parameter is selected by the Newey and West (1994) procedure

The J-statistic is the test for validity of overidentifying restrictions, and numbers within parentheses are p-values. The Cragg-Donald F-statistic is the test for the null hypothesis of weak instruments, and the critical values are tabulated in Stock and Yogo (2002)

**indicates significance at the 5% level

can check the validity of the theoretical results under the condition that $\sigma < 1$. This result is consistent with the findings of previous studies based on micro data (e.g., Oberfield and Raval 2014).

4.2 Estimation of Efficiency Coefficients *A* and *B*

Since it is empirically found that the elasticity of substitution between capital and labor is less than 1, our concern is for the validity of the theoretical results under the condition that $\sigma < 1$. In this section, we examine whether technological progress in Japan had bias according to the classification of Proposition 1.1. This proposition states the following:

Proposition 1.1 *When the elasticity of substitution between capital and labor is less than 1, technological progress is labor-saving or capital-saving, depending on whether the growth rate of the capital efficiency coefficient B_t is negative or positive.*

To examine the type of technological progress in Japan, we examine the dynamics of B_t, which can be calculated from Eq. (4.9). For this purpose, we use the data from the Cabinet Office because of data availability issues (see Sect. 4.1.2). The sample period is from 1994 to 2015. The capital service index (corporations) is used as a measure of K_t, and its corresponding price index is used as a measure of r_t.[2] The data on total earnings per man-hour and the man-hour index are used as measures of w_t and N_t, respectively. For the man-hour index, data from the RIETI are used until 2012, and data from the Monthly Labor Survey are used after 2013. Aggregate output Y_t and its price are measured by real GDP and the GDP deflator. All data are standardized (2011 = 100).

Taking the exponential of Eq. (4.9), we obtain time series observations of B_t. For reference purposes, we also calculate A_t using Eq. (4.10). We follow Sato (1970) and standardize the initial values of A_t and B_t to 1 because their data units are different. The results are reported in Fig. 4.1. It is clear that the time trend of B_t is negative. Actually, the average growth rate of B_t for the sample period is −3.7%. Therefore, this empirical result suggests that technological progress in Japan after the 1990s has been predominantly labor-saving.

On the other hand, the average growth rate of A_t for the sample period is 2.0%. This result is consistent with the assumption in Chap. 1.

[2]These observations are reported as reference series. For details, see the following site. http://www.esri.cao.go.jp/jp/sna/data/data_list/capital-service/index.html.

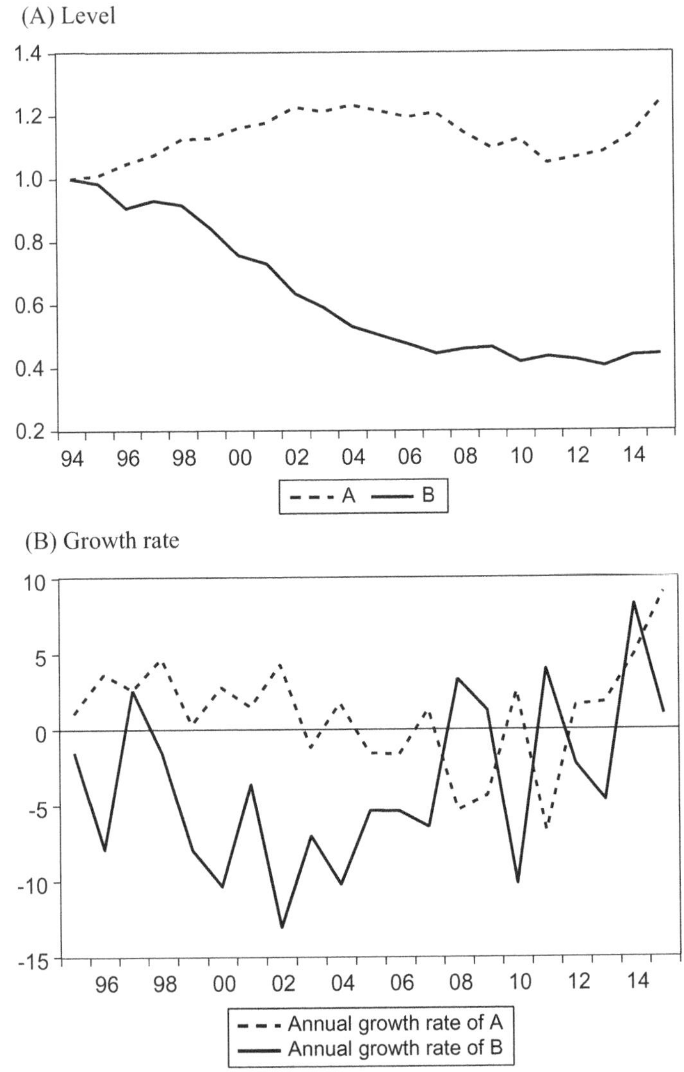

Fig. 4.1 Dynamics of *A* and *B*

4.3 Introduction of Biased Technology

Using the estimation results for B_t, we can extend the empirical investigation in Sect. 4.2. Specifically, the conditions for the introduction of biased technology are characterized as follows:

Proposition 1.4 *If the labor share of income is higher than the elasticity of substitution between capital and labor, labor-saving technology is introduced and the growth* *rate of the efficiency coefficient of capital is negative. However, if the labor share of income is smaller than the elasticity of substitution, capital-saving technology is introduced and the growth rate of the efficiency coefficient of capital is positive.*

To examine the validity of this proposition, we use a simple regression model

$$B_t - B_{t-1} = b_0 + b_1 \frac{1}{j} \sum_{i=1}^{j} (x_{t-i} - \sigma), \quad j = 1, 2, 3, \tag{4.11}$$

where x_t is the labor share of income, and b_0 and b_1 are the parameters. We use the sample mean of the labor share of income because we expect that firms consider economic conditions over a few years when deciding on the introduction of new technology. The theoretical result suggests that $b_1 < 0$.

The data on the labor share of income is obtained from the RIETI, and the sample period is from 1994 to 2012. The end of the sample period is determined because data on the labor share of income is available until 2012. The estimation results for Eq. (4.11) are reported in Table 4.5. We find that b_1 is significantly negative at conventional levels for all cases. Therefore, the proposition holds in Japan. Our empirical evidence that the labor share of income with three lags (average) has higher significance can be interpreted as suggesting that the introduction of new technology is decided after considering economic conditions over a few years.

The graphical interpretation of Eq. (4.11) is presented in Fig. 4.2. Data on the labor share of income is smoothed after taking the average of its lagged values, suggesting that the average values reflect a medium- and long-term trend. We find that the annual change in B_t is negatively associated with the labor share of income (expressed as the difference in the elasticity of substitution), especially for the period from the late 1990s to the late 2000s.

Table 4.5 Estimation results of Eq. (4.11)

Parameter	Estimate	Standard error
(A) Explanatory variable: $x_{t-1} - \sigma$		
b_0	–0.026*	0.014
b_1	–0.716*	0.419
(B) Explanatory variable: $\frac{1}{2} \sum_{i=1}^{2} (x_{t-i} - \sigma)$		
b_0	–0.026**	0.012
b_1	–0.666*	0.377
(C) Explanatory variable: $\frac{1}{3} \sum_{i=1}^{3} (x_{t-i} - \sigma)$		
b_0	–0.025**	0.011
b_1	–0.767**	0.378

HAC standard errors are reported
** and *indicate significance at the 5% and 10% levels, respectively

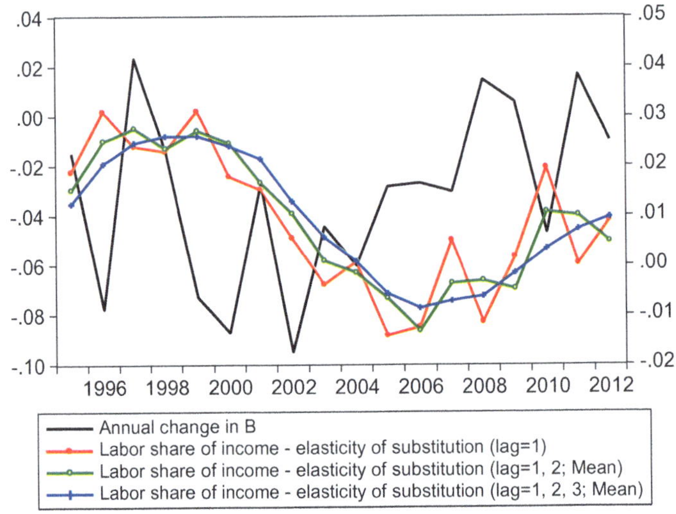

Fig. 4.2 Graphical interpretation for Eq. (4.11) Left scale: Annual change in B_t Right scale: Labor share of income−elasticity of substitution

4.4 Interpretation for the Dynamics of the Labor Share of Income

Given that labor-saving technological progress is introduced under the condition $\sigma < 1$, the following proposition is derived:

Proposition 1.5 *The labor share of income tends to decrease if it is greater than the elasticity of substitution between capital and labor, and vice versa. Consequently, the labor share of income is adjusted toward the value of the elasticity of substitution in the long run.*

In this section, the validity of this proposition is empirically examined in two ways: (i) graphical analysis and (ii) estimation of an error correction model.

4.4.1 Graphical Analysis

Figure 4.3 indicates the labor share of income, which is calculated using the data from the RIETI. We find that the labor share of income in Japan is adjusted toward the elasticity of substitution between labor and capital over the sample period. The labor share of income was much higher than the elasticity of substitution in the late 1970s but declined very quickly from the 1980s. After the 1990s, this variable fluctuated stably around the value of the elasticity of substitution.

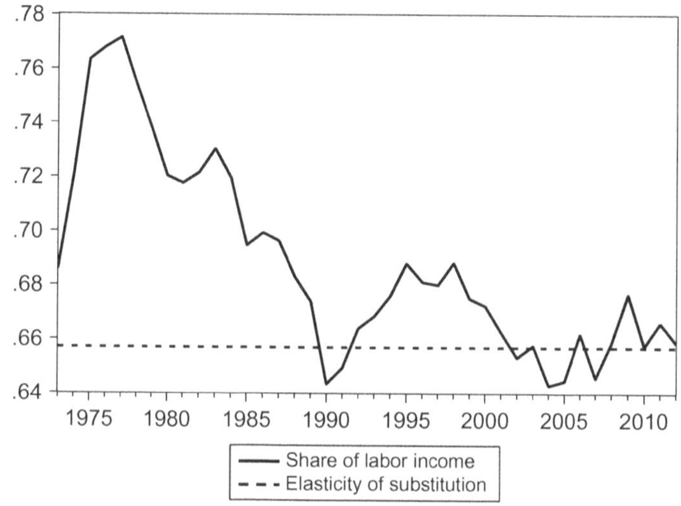

Fig. 4.3 Labor share of income and the elasticity of substitution between capital and labor

4.4.2 Estimation of Error Correction Model

The graphical analysis suggests that the relationship between the labor share of income and the elasticity of substitution is consistent with the theoretical result. To assess this relationship more accurately, we estimate a simple error correction model as

$$x_t - x_{t-1} = \alpha_0 + \alpha_1 \frac{1}{j} \sum_{i=1}^{j} (x_{t-i} - \sigma), \quad j = 1, 2, 3 \tag{4.12}$$

where x_t is the labor share of income, and α_0 and α_1 are the parameters. The explanatory variable is the same as in the analysis in Sect. 4.3.

The theoretical result suggests that $\alpha_1 < 0$ and $\alpha_0 = 0$. The former condition means the existence of an error correction mechanism, and the equilibrium value is σ. The latter condition implies that the labor share of income does not change when its value is equal to σ. The sample period is from 1994 to 2012, which is consistent with the analysis in Sect. 4.3. The data are expressed in percentage terms, and the estimated value of σ (65.7; Table 4.4) is used to estimate Eq. (4.12).

The estimation results are reported in Table 4.6. We find that α_0 is not significant and α_1 is significantly negative. Therefore, there is empirical evidence that the labor share of income fluctuates stably around the equilibrium value σ.

Table 4.6 Error correction mechanism of labor share of income

Parameter	Estimate	Standard error
(A) Explanatory variable: $x_{t-1} - \sigma$		
α_0	0.222	0.243
α_1	-0.352*	0.178
(B) Explanatory variable: $\frac{1}{2}\sum_{i=1}^{2}(x_{t-i} - \sigma)$		
α_0	0.093	0.213
α_1	-0.304**	0.142
(C) Explanatory variable: $\frac{1}{3}\sum_{i=1}^{3}(x_{t-i} - \sigma)$		
α_0	0.055	0.153
α_1	-0.235*	0.125

HAC standard errors are reported
** and *indicate significance at the 5% and 10% levels, respectively

4.5 Empirical Analysis of a Trade-off Between Types of Technological Progress

The empirical analysis in Sect. 4.2 suggests that B_t has a trend opposite that of A_t (Fig. 4.1). This result is consistent with a key assumption in Chap. 2 as follows:

Assumption (Chap. 2). *A trade-off exists between the rates of labor-augmenting technological progress and capital-augmenting technological progress (i.e., the innovation possibility frontier).*

Figure 4.4 indicates the scatter diagram of the annual growth rates of A_t and B_t, and the fitted line is obtained from a second polynomial regression.[3] This result suggests that the assumption of the innovation possibility frontier holds in Japan.

4.6 Effects of Technological Progress on Unemployment

Finally, we examine the effect of technological progress on unemployment. Since the unemployment rate is equal to one minus the employment rate, the theoretical result shown in Chap. 3 is rewritten as follows:

Proposition 3.4 *If the labor share of income is higher than the elasticity of substitution between labor and capital, labor-saving innovation is adopted and the unemployment rate increases. However, if the labor share of income is smaller than the elasticity of substitution, capital-saving innovation is adopted and the unemployment rate decreases.*

[3]The observations in 1997, 1998, 2014, and 2015 are excluded from this figure because they are clearly outliers. However, using a dummy variable technique, we find that the growth rate of A_t is significantly and negatively associated with the growth rate of B_t.

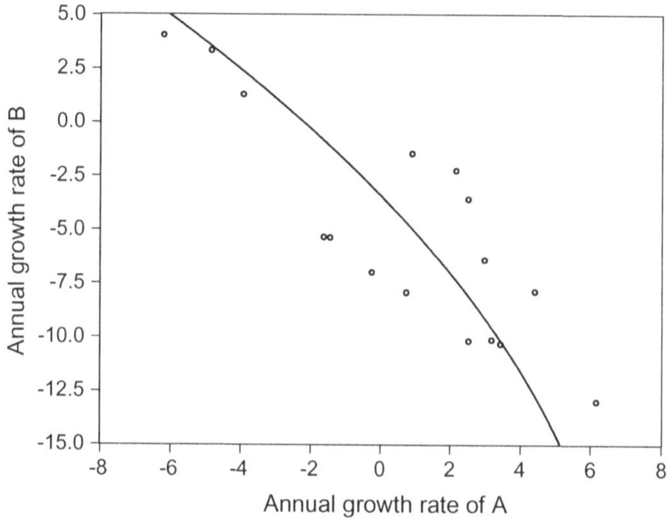

Fig. 4.4 Scatter diagram of the annual growth rates of A_t and B_t

To check the empirical validity of this proposition, we use the regression model as

$$u_t - u_{t-1} = \gamma_0 + \gamma_1 \frac{1}{j} \sum_{i=1}^{j} (x_{t-i} - \sigma), \quad j = 1, 2, 3 \tag{4.13}$$

where u_t denotes the unemployment rate; x_t, the labor share of income; σ, the elasticity of substitution between capital and labor; and γ_0, γ_1, the coefficients. The explanatory variable is the same as in the analysis in Sect. 4.3.

The sample period is from 1994 to 2012, which is consistent with the analysis in Sect. 4.3. The data on the unemployment rate are obtained from the OECD, and we assume that $\sigma = 0.657$ (65.7%) based on the estimation results reported in Table 4.4. All data are expressed in percentage terms.

The estimation results for Eq. (4.13) are reported in Table 4.7. We find that γ_1 is significantly positive for all cases, suggesting that the unemployment rate increases as the labor share of income is higher than the elasticity of substitution between labor and capital. Therefore, the proposition is empirically supported by the Japanese data.

The graphical interpretation of Eq. (4.13) is indicated in Fig. 4.5. We find that the annual change in the unemployment rate is positively associated with the labor share of income (expressed as the difference from the elasticity of substitution) over the sample period. This result suggests that the unemployment rate is affected by the introduction of new technology over short-, medium-, and long-term periods.

Table 4.7 Estimation results for unemployment equations

Parameter	Estimate	Standard error
(A) Explanatory variable: $x_{t-1} - \sigma$		
γ_0	–0.067	0.054
γ_1	0.200***	0.038
(B) Explanatory variable: $\frac{1}{2}\sum_{i=1}^{2}(x_{t-i} - \sigma)$		
γ_0	–0.079	0.048
γ_1	0.197***	0.035
(C) Explanatory variable: $\frac{1}{3}\sum_{i=1}^{3}(x_{t-i} - \sigma)$		
γ_0	–0.065	0.042
γ_1	0.176***	0.026

HAC standard errors are reported
***indicates significance at the 1%, level

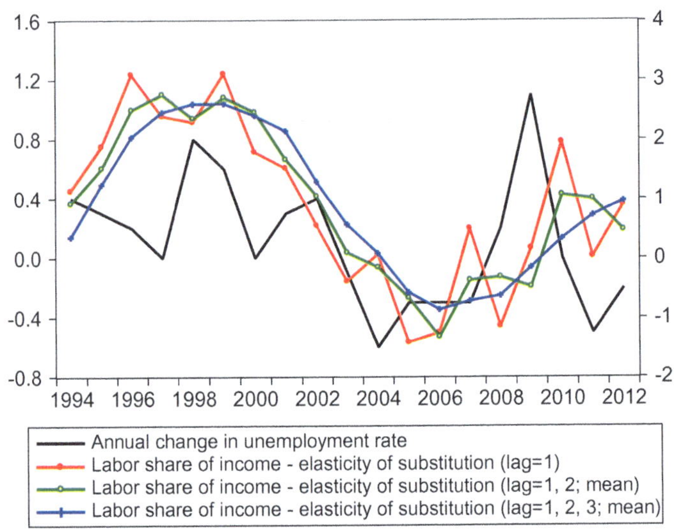

Fig. 4.5 Graphical interpretation for Eq. (4.13) Left scale: Annual change in the unemployment rate (%) Right scale: Labor share of income−elasticity of substitution (%)

4.7 Conclusions

For the first time in the literature, we empirically examine the macroeconomic impact of innovation on the basis of the efficiency coefficient of capital B. In particular, it is noteworthy that the growth rate of B is negative on average over the sample period. We show that this result can be interpreted as evidence suggesting that labor-saving technological progress is introduced. Furthermore, the classification of the types of innovation is extended to the empirical analysis of the determinants of the unemployment rate, and we find that the adoption of labor-saving innovation increases the unemployment rate. Key factors for these analyses are the labor share of income and the elasticity of substitution between capital and labor. This chapter proposes a new estimation procedure for the elasticity of substitution; its estimation result is similar to the results reported in previous studies. Therefore, fluctuations of B calculated based on this parameter appear to be plausible. Although B tends to decrease until the late 2000s, its level remains almost unchanged in recent years as shown in Sect. 4.2. Hence, it is important to examine future dynamics of B using the same approach as in this chapter.

Chapter 5
Concluding Remarks

5.1 Interpretation of the Results

This volume has focused on investigating the influence of technological progress on the distribution of income between labor and capital, as well as on the unemployment rate, concentrating specifically on the role of biased technological progress. Canonical growth models, both exogenous and endogenous, have most often been used to analyze the properties of the steady state equilibrium, assuming technological progress to be neutral. This is because the properties of the steady state equilibrium attained under neutral technological progress can consistently explain the so-called "stylized facts of capitalist development" that represent broad historical constancies of macroeconomic variables such as the capital/output ratio, labor share of income, and rate of return on capital. However, by analyzing long-run empirical data that are extensive both in periods and number of countries, Piketty (2014) finds that these macroeconomic variables do not remain constant but secularly alternate phases of rising and falling. In particular, by examining the annual changes in the eight wealthiest countries for the period between 1970 and 2010 with reliable and homogeneous data for the capital/income ratio and capital share of income, he shows that both variables have an upward trend in the long-run, with fluctuations in the short-run.

Among a number of factors contributing to the secular increase in the capital share of income (the secular decrease in the labor share of income) and the resulting increase in income inequality in these periods, two that are regarded as important are globalization and technological progress. First, globalization causes advanced countries to face increased competition from countries where wages of unskilled workers are low, which increases the demand for skilled workers as the balance of production shifts towards high-skill sectors. As a result, it is argued that wage inequality between skilled and unskilled workers increases, while the labor share of income decreases. Second, technological progress in recent years is considered to be skill-biased and labor-saving, which creates increases in wage inequality between skilled and unskilled labor, and decreases in the labor share of income. Out of these

H. Adachi et al., *Technological Progress, Income Distribution, and Unemployment*,
Kobe University Social Science Research Series,
https://doi.org/10.1007/978-981-13-3726-0_5

two factors, this volume has focused on technological progress that has tended to have a labor-saving bias in recent years and analyzed its effects on income distribution and unemployment.

Technological change is not given exogenously like "manna from heaven" but is derived endogenously from decisions that are made by scientists, governments, businessmen, consumers, and others. In this volume, we have focused on firms' decisions about the choice of an innovation type and analyzed the implications for growth, income distribution, and unemployment. The firm's decision to choose the degree of bias in technological change was originally formulated in models of induced innovation developed by Kennedy (1964), Drandakis and Phelps (1965), and others in the 1960s. Those models assumed that firms select from a menu on the innovation possibility frontier so as to maximize their cost reduction rate.

In contrast to those models, the model we developed in Chap. 2 of this volume assumed that firms select from the menu so as to maximize the discounted value of their expected profits, which is a natural way of formulating firms' behaviors. With this assumption, it was shown that if the labor share of income is larger than the elasticity of substitution between labor and capital, firms decide to introduce labor-saving innovation in Harrod's sense. Under this sense of labor-saving innovation, however, the efficiency of labor rises, while the efficiency of capital falls, and hence, the capital/output ratio increases and the labor share of income decreases (the capital share of income increases). The directions of changes in these macroeconomic variables coincide with Piketty's (2014) empirical results. This implies that labor-saving technological progress can be a promising factor for explaining the long-run macroeconomic trend observed in advanced countries since the 1970s. Furthermore, as we have shown in Chap. 3, if we incorporate the wage setting equation, which can be derived from the efficiency wage hypothesis or wage bargaining hypothesis, into the neoclassical growth model, the unemployment rate is endogenously determined, and labor-saving technological progress leads to a higher rate of unemployment. Hence, labor-saving innovation may also explain the long-lasting high unemployment rate in some advanced countries since the 1970s.

What are the welfare implications of firms' profit maximizing decisions for the market outcomes represented by the degree of bias in innovation, income distribution, and the unemployment rate? As we have shown in Chaps. 2 and 3, compared to the social welfare maximizing level, the innovation type determined in markets is more labor-saving, and hence the long-run labor share of income is lower, and the long-run unemployment rate is higher. In other words, the market is inefficient in the sense that it produces neither the socially optimal pattern of innovation nor the socially optimal share of income and unemployment rate. This implies that some relevant policies are required to improve social welfare. We will discuss this later.

This volume has dealt with factor income distribution (e.g., income distribution between labor and capital), but not with personal income distribution. The problem is whether any relationship exists between the two. Does a fall (rise) in the labor share of income mean that personal income distribution becomes more (less) unequal? If workers only receive wage income and no income from wealth, a fall in the labor share of income will lead to more unequal personal income distribution, because the income level of wealth owners is usually higher than that of workers. Today, in contrast, a person who earns wages may also receive interest on savings and benefits from owning a house. In this case, a fall in the labor share of income may not result in more unequal personal income distribution. However, in an empirical study of sixteen OECD countries from 1970 to 1996, Checchi and Garcia-Penalosa (2010) showed that a 1% point rise in the labor share of income is associated with a 0.7% point decline in the Gini coefficient. Thus, based on their empirical research, we may conclude that the falling tendency in the labor share of income from the 1970s through the present is one of the factors that has increased inequality in personal income distribution.

5.2 Policy Implications and Further Research

Several policy implications can be derived from our analyses. First, as pointed out by Stiglitz (2014), wage subsidies can be an effective way of increasing the labor share of income and employment in the medium run or long run. As mentioned above, firms' profit maximizing decisions lead to more labor-saving innovation compared to the social welfare maximizing level. Firms choose labor-saving innovation when the labor share of income (=labor costs per unit of output) is relatively too high. Thus, to induce firms to choose less labor-saving innovation, firms' labor costs must be reduced. Wage subsidies reduce firms' burden of labor costs, and thus induce firms to choose less labor-saving technology, which leads to increases in the labor share of income and decreases in the unemployment rate. On the contrary, a fall in the cost of capital due to a low interest rate policy, for example, encourages labor-saving innovation, and as a result employment will decrease in the medium run or long run through substitution of labor with capital. In the short run, however, a fall in the cost of capital has the effect of increasing employment through increased aggregate demand, since it encourages investment. There are intertemporal trade-offs between these two effects, but analyzing the net results is beyond the scope of this volume.

Second, we can think of a policy that combines an environmental tax, such as a carbon tax, with a tax credit depending on the number of workers hired by the firm to maintain or enhance employability at firms. This mixed policy may induce firms to shift the direction of innovation towards a less labor-saving one. Thus, it would have favorable effects not only on the environment but also on income distribution and employment.

Third, instead of using the market mechanism to control the direction of innovation through taxes and/or subsidies, the government can directly influence the direction of technological change. Concerning this type of public policy, Atkinson's (2015, Chap. 4) proposal is worth noting. According to him, the government can directly influence the direction of technological change not only by financing scientific research, but also through licensing, regulating, and educating. Indeed, a lot of technologies that are currently used in firms and industries come from fundamental research supported by governments. As an example, Atkinson (2015, p. 119) refers to the case of the iPhone, which depended on seven or eight fundamental scientific and technological breakthroughs supported by U.S. government funding. If, as this case illustrates, the government can influence the direction of technological change, the government should consider not only efficiency but also the implications for income distribution and employment when making decisions about supporting innovation. From this point of view, Atkinson (2015, pp. 121–123) recommends investment for technological advancement in a public sector that is characterized as labor-intensive with low productivity. Investment in infrastructure, like roads or airports, is such an example, but what he regards as more important is investment in human capital, including investment in services and facilities for children and improving the quality of formal education. Such investment in human capital may improve intergenerational equity. He also points out the importance of investment in improving public administration. This is because, as he says, "*the achievement of an equitable society depends to a considerable degree on the effectiveness of the public administration and the quality of its dealing with citizens*" (Atkinson 2015, p. 122).

Last, we point out two directions for developing our research. First, for further analysis of inequality, it may be more desirable to extend our model to include skill-biased technological progress. This volume analyzed influences of biased technological progress on income distribution and unemployment, using an aggregate growth model that includes only two factors of production: labor and capital. Since labor is homogeneous in our model, we have not dealt with skill-biased technological progress, which is regarded as having played an important role in generating wage inequality in recent years. In this respect, Stiglitz (2014) suggests a promising research direction. Second, there appears to be growing literature concerning the influence of AI robots on future income distribution and unemployment. Among others, Summers (2013), Korineck and Stiglitz (2017), and Berg et al. (2017) suggest interesting models for analyzing this problem. However, research in this field has just begun, and is worth developing further.

References

Acemoglu, D. (2003). Labor- and capital-augmenting technical change. *Journal of the European Economic Association, 1*(1), 1–37.

Acemoglu, D. (2010). When does labor scarcity encourage innovation? *Journal of Political Economy, 118*(6), 1037–1078.

Acemoglu, D. (2015). Localized and biased technologies: Atkinson and Stiglitz's new view, induced innovations, and directed technological change. *Economic Journal, 125,* 443–457.

Acemoglu, D., Autor, D., Dorn, D., Hanson, G. H., & Price, B. (2014). Return to the Solow paradox? IT, productivity, and employment in US manufacturing. *American Economic Review: Papers and Proceedings, 104*(5), 394–399.

Acemoglu, D., & Restrepo, P. (2017). Robots and jobs: Evidence from US labor markets. NBER Working Papers, 23285, National Bureau of Economic Research.

Acemoglu, D., & Restrepo, P. (2018). The race between man and machine: Implications of technology for growth, factor shares and employment. *American Economic Review, 108*(6), 1488–1542.

Adachi, H. (2009). Unemployment and income distribution in the medium-run growth model. *Advances in Mathematical Economics, 12,* 1–24.

Aghion, P., & Howitt, P. (1994). Growth and employment. *Review of Economic Studies, 61*(3), 477–494.

Autor, D., & Salomons, A. (2017). Robocalypse now—Does productivity growth threaten employment? Paper Prepared for the ECB Forum on Central Banking.

Ahmad, S. (1966). On the theory of induced innovation. *Economic Journal, 76,* 344–357.

Berg, A., Buffie, E., & Zanna, F. (2017). Should we fear the robot revolution? (The Correct Answer is Yes). International Monetary Fund.

Blanchard, O. J. (1997). Medium run. *Brooking Papers on Economic Activity, 28*(2), 89–158.

Blume, L. E., & Durlauf, S. N. (2015). Capital in the twenty-first century: A review essay. *Journal of Political Economy, 123*(4), 749–777.

Checchi, D., & Penerosa, C. G. (2010). Labour market institutions and personal distribution of income in the OECD. *Economica, 77,* 413–450.

Chirinko, R. S. (2008). Sigma: The long and short of it. *Journal of Macroeconomics, 30,* 671–686.

Chirinko, R. S., & Mallick, D. (2017). The substitution elasticity, factor shares, and low frequency panel model. *American Economic Journal: Macroeconomics, 9*(4), 225–253.

Drandakis, E. M., & Phelps, E. S. (1966). A model of induced invention, growth, and distribution. *Economic Journal, 76,* 823–840.

Grossman, G. M., Helpman, E., Oberfield, E., & Sampson, T. (2017). Balanced growth despite Uzawa. *American Economic Review, 107*(4), 1293–1312.

H. Adachi et al., *Technological Progress, Income Distribution, and Unemployment*, Kobe University Social Science Research Series,
https://doi.org/10.1007/978-981-13-3726-0

Hansen, L. P. (1982). Large sample properties of generalized method of moments estimators. *Econometrica, 50,* 1029–1054.

Harrod, R. F. (1948). *Towards a dynamic economics.* London: Macmillan.

Homburg, S. (2015). Critical remarks on Piketty's Capital in the twenty-first century. *Applied Economics, 47*(14), 1401–1406.

Jones, C. I. (2016). The facts of economic growth. In J. Taylor & H. Uhlig (Eds.), *Handbook of macroeconomics* (Vol. 2). Amsterdam: Elsevier.

Jorgenson, D. W. (1963). Capital theory and investment behavior. *American Economic Review, 53* (2), 247–259.

Kaldor, N. (1961). Capital accumulation and economic growth. In F. A. Lutz & D. C. Hague (Eds.), *The theory of capital.* New York: St. Martin's Press.

Kennedy, C. (1964). Induced bias in innovation and the theory of distribution. *Economic Journal, 74,* 541–547.

Korinek, A., & Stiglitz, J. E. (2017). Artificial intelligence and implications for income distribution and unemployment. NBER Working Paper, 24174, National Bureau of Economic Research.

Kuznets, S. (1955). Economic growth and income inequality. *American Economic Review, 45*(1), 1–28.

Lawrence, R. Z. (2015). Recent declines in labor's share in US income. NBER Working Papers, 21269, National Bureau of Economic Research.

Layard, R., Nickell, S., & Jackman, R. (2005). *Unemployment: Macroeconomic performance and the labor market.* Oxford University Press.

Newey, W., & West, K. (1994). Automatic lag selection in covariance matrix estimation. *Review of Economic Studies, 61,* 631–653.

Nordhaus, W. D. (1973). Some skeptical thoughts on the theory of induced innovation. *Quarterly Journal of Economics, 87,* 208–219.

Oberfield, E., & Raval, D. (2014). Micro data and macro technology. NBER Working Papers, 20452. National Bureau of Economic Research.

Phillips, P. C. B., & Perron, P. (1988). Testing for a unit root in time series regression. *Biometrica, 75,* 335–346.

Pianta, M. (2006). Innovation and employment (Chap. 21). In *The Oxford handbook of innovation* (pp. 568–598). Oxford University Press.

Piketty, T. (2014). *Capital in the twenty-first century.* Cambridge, Massachusetts: Belknap Press of Harvard University Press.

Robinson, J (1956). *Accumulation of Capital,* Palgrave Macmillan.

Samuelson, P. (1966). A theory of induced innovation along Kennedy-Weizacker lines. *Review of Economics and Statistics, 33,* 133–146.

Sato, R. (1970). The estimation of biased technical progress and the production function. *International Economic Review, 11,* 179–208.

Sato, R., & Morita, T. (2009). Quantity and quality: The impact of labour saving innovation on US and Japanese growth rates, 1960–2004. *Japanese Economic Review, 60,* 407–434.

Solow, R. (1956). A contribution to the theory of economic growth. *Quarterly Journal of Economics, 70,* 65–94.

Solow, R. (1987). We'd better watch out. *New York Times Book Review,* July 12.

Stiglitz, J. E. (2014). Unemployment and innovation. NBER Working Paper, 20670, National Bureau of Economic Research.

Stock, J. H., & Yogo, M. (2002). Testing for weak instruments in linear IV regression. NBER Technical Working Paper, 0284, National Bureau of Economic Research.

Summers, L. H. (2013). Economic possibilities for our children. The 2013 Martin Feldstein Lecture. *NBER Reporter, 4,* 1–6.

Summers, L. H. (2014). The inequality puzzle. *Democracy: A Journal of Ideas, 32,* Spring.

Vanek, J. (1966). Towards a more general theory of growth with technological change. *Economic Journal, 76,* 841–854.

The manufacturer's authorised representative in the EU is Springer Nature Customer Service Centre GmbH, Europaplatz 3, 69115 Heidelberg, Germany. If you have any concerns regarding our products, please contact ProductSafety@springernature.com

Printed and bound by CPI Group (UK) Ltd, Croydon, CR0 4YY
25/09/2026
02222891-0014